Contents

Executive Summary

This report examines a widely known and recognized issue that has rarely been explored systematically: how state laws, policies, and practices affect the course of urban revitalization—the process by which a municipality takes steps to improve its economic, physical, and social condition. The ability of American cities to revitalize and the ways by which they do so are closely interwoven with—and often determined by—the laws, policies, and practices of state governments, which exercise overt or latent control over almost every significant local government activity. From the way cities raise operating revenues to the conditions under which they can finance redevelopment projects, that control is baked into the American political system and unlikely to change in the foreseeable future.

The rebranding of South Broad Street in Philadelphia, Pennsylvania, into the Avenue of the Arts has helped transform it to a major draw for visitors and an economic engine for the city. *Source: Paul Sableman/Flickr.*

This has two powerful implications for policy and action. First, state leaders must take constructive, responsible steps to change laws and practices that work against the revival of small and large urban centers and to ensure that any revival benefits the entire city, particularly its lower-income residents and communities of color, rather than only its elites. Second, advocates for urban revitalization need to pay more attention to state government. While federal government and its vast resources will never be irrelevant, the panoply of states' legal powers and policy tools make states the key players after the cities themselves in fostering urban revival. When those seeking change understand the state's role, they can better identify opportunities for change and become more effective advocates for state policies that foster inclusive, equitable revitalization of their state's cities and towns.

This report specifically explores the state's role in urban revitalization and explicitly considers equity in revitalization. Much of the urban revival of the past two decades has led to more inequality and polarization, both racial and economic; future revitalization efforts must explicitly design for more equitable outcomes.

It is important to recognize that urban revitalization is not a single activity or outcome; rather, it is the sum of a series of ongoing processes taking place simultaneously in five distinct but interrelated sectors:

- Strong fiscal capacity and service delivery.
- A robust real estate market.
- A competitive economy.
- Healthy neighborhoods and quality of life.
- Human capital development.

While each of these elements requires separate strategies and investments, they interact with and reinforce one another. Without the economic competitiveness that can enable the city to grow jobs and businesses or the quality of life that makes the city an attractive place to live and work, the ability to maximize human capital for the benefit of the city is sharply reduced. Each of these is discussed in detail in chapters 4 and 5.

Inclusion, or the extent to which revitalization benefits all of the people of the city, must be part of that equation. That means not only taking concrete steps to distribute benefits fairly but also ensuring that residents who have been historically excluded from participation in important decisions can actively share in those decisions going forward. Given the powerful tendency of market-based strategies to favor those people who are already successful, however, a policy that is economically neutral typically perpetuates inequitable outcomes. Intentional strategies are necessary for ensuring equitable ends. Moreover, if public strategies for more inclusive or equitable growth are to be established, state policy will have to play a central role.

> When those seeking change understand the state's role, they can better identify opportunities for change and become more effective advocates for state policies that foster inclusive, equitable revitalization of their state's cities and towns.

State policies that actively further equitable, inclusive revitalization at the local level can both support municipalities seeking to infuse greater equity into their revitalization and move reluctant actors in that direction. Likewise, the absence of such explicit policies will inevitably undermine local efforts at inclusion and equity and likely empower those hostile or indifferent to such efforts, too. Inclusion is not a challenge that exists apart from the elements of revitalization described earlier—it is instead a way to design the ground rules that govern those elements more conscientiously.

In 2011, the Michigan legislature enacted a regressive charter school law that unintentionally but measurably harmed low-income students in Detroit. *Source: Jim West/Alamy Stock Photo.*

It does not take deliberate intent to exacerbate inequality. Many laws are enacted with little aware-ness of unintended consequences, and, once on the books, they tend to stay there. We do not believe that Michigan's notoriously regressive charter school law was enacted with deliberate intent to harm Detroit's struggling low-income children, for example, but it has had that effect, which could easily have been predicted. Although those results have become apparent since the early 2010s and despite repeated calls for reform since 2016, the state has taken no action to change those policies or mitigate their inequitable outcomes.

While specific proposals for how states can advance urban revitalization will vary based on the needs of their cities and on the state's political culture and fis-cal climate, advocates should ground their proposals in five underlying principles:

- Target areas of greatest need instead of pursuing "place-neutral" policies.

- Think regionally by recognizing and addressing the connections between cities and their regions to foster regional thinking and redress inequities.

- Break down silos to establish and improve relationships among different areas and governmental roles at both the state and local levels.

- Support cities' own efforts to take responsibility for the future, rather than attempt to substitute state mandates or direction for local efforts.

- Build in equity and inclusivity into all state policies and programs.

Fostering equitable revitalization requires both a broad, principled commitment and concrete steps to that end. As with most things, the devil is in the details. This report provides detailed recommenda-tions designed to lead state governments to become true partners with their cities in bringing about inclu-sive, equitable revitalization.

CHAPTER 1
Introduction

Thanks to state support, the Cap at Union Station on High Street bridges I-670 in Columbus, Ohio, to connect the city's downtown with the Short North neighborhood. *Source: Division 7 Roofing, Columbus, Ohio.*

The ways in which state laws, policies, and practices affect the course of urban revitalization—the process by which a city or town takes steps to improve its economic, physical and social conditions—are widely known and recognized yet seldom explored substantially. While every local government has these concerns, older cities of the United States share a particular interest—especially legacy cities, the primarily midwestern and northeastern cities that have lost their peak populations and industrial economies. Despite some revival in the past decade or two, such places are still struggling to regain their former prosperity and to provide residents with opportunity and decent quality of life (Mallach and Brachman 2013).

State governments exercise overt or latent control over almost every significant local government activity, from the way they raise operating revenues to the conditions under which they can finance redevelopment projects. Their control is baked into the American political system and is not likely to change in the foreseeable future. American cities' ability to rebuild their economic, physical, and social environments—and the ways through which they can do so—are often closely interwoven with and determined by the laws, policies, and practices of their state governments.

This has two powerful implications for policy and action. First, assuming most state leaders are eager to enhance the social, fiscal, and physical health and vitality of their older cities and towns, they must understand how current laws and practices affect those places and recognize that many policies with the greatest impacts on urban revitalization are not overtly about urban revitalization at all. They must also take constructive, responsible steps to change laws and practices that work against the revival of small and large urban centers and ensure that any revival equitably benefits the entire city, particularly its lower-income residents and communities of color.

Second, urban revitalization advocates need to pay more attention to state government. Federal government with its vast resources will never be irrelevant—least of all today, when federal stimulus funding has been a lifeline for states and cities across the country in the wake of the coronavirus pandemic. Yet the panoply of states' legal powers and policy tools make states the key players after the cities themselves in

Ybor City in Tampa, Florida, was once the cigar-making capital of the United States; today, the neighborhood is a National Register Historic District and Tampa's greatest tourist attraction. *Source: VisionsbyAtlee/iStock/Getty Images Plus.*

The Maggie L. Walker Memorial Plaza in the Jackson Ward neighborhood of Richmond, Virginia, celebrates an early twentieth century leader in the area through a community-driven public space. *Source: Emory Minnick Photography.*

fostering urban revival. When those seeking change understand the state's role, they may better identify opportunities for change and become more effective advocates for state policies that foster inclusive, equitable revitalization of their state's cities and towns.

While the issues raised in this report are longstanding, they have taken on a particular urgency recently amid the still-unpredictable effects of the COVID-19 pandemic, along with the massive one-time infusion of funds from the American Rescue Plan to state capitols and city halls across the country. Whether and how we take advantage of those resources—and potentially even greater resources in the future under forthcoming federal infrastructure programs—will affect our cities for years to come.

This report is specifically about the state's role in urban revitalization. States also play a major and widely varying part in supporting what can be called urban subsistence—that is, the day-to-day ability of a city to function and of its residents to survive. Supporting that subsistence is invaluable, yet it should not be conflated with policies designed to further cities' ability to rebuild their physical, social, and economic environments, or to thwart their efforts to do so. This report addresses revitalization, not subsistence. What revitalization means is addressed in chapter 2.

This report is also explicitly about equity in urban revitalization. Much of the recent urban revival in the United States has led to more inequality and polarization, both racial and economic, than equity and opportunity. This is not by chance. As scholar-activist Ibram X. Kendi has written, "There is no such thing as a nonracist or race-neutral policy. Every policy in every institution in every community is producing or sustaining either racial inequity or equity" (2019). If future revitalization efforts are to lead to more equitable outcomes, they must explicitly design for those outcomes.

These issues are not limited to large cities or metropolitan centers. The challenges of urban revitalization—economic competitiveness, market vitality, and building human capital—are faced by large and small cities, as well as by many towns, including many inner-ring suburbs of larger cities. Indeed, smaller municipalities often face even greater challenges than major ones, because they may lack the economic engines of larger places and may be more limited in local capacity and organizational infrastructure.

This report provides a clear picture of how state laws and practices help or hinder equitable urban revitalization. It should help guide state policy makers to evaluate their own laws and policies and encourage more effective advocacy for changes in state laws and policies, with the goal of bringing about more sustainable, inclusive revival of our older cities and towns. If there is one central message in this report, it is that states matter—and that those who care about the future of our cities need to direct far greater attention to them.

CHAPTER 2
How States Control Cities

Above all, states matter because of the overt or latent control they exert over municipalities subject to their jurisdiction, to the point that almost any activity a city may pursue to further revitalization is either dependent on or powerfully affected by its state government. The legal and fiscal basis for state control ultimately underlies the many ways in which state government helps—or hinders—urban revitalization.

Iowa Supreme Court Justice John F. Dillon's conception of the relationship between states and municipalities has defined an ongoing tug-of-war in legislatures across the country, including Iowa's own. *Source: Phil Roeder/Flickr.*

The Legal Framework

The dominant role of the state in municipal governance has long been reflected in the concept that municipalities are "creatures of the state." Although Iowa Supreme Court Justice John F. Dillon did not originate the phrase, his 1868 definition of the relationship between states and municipalities in *Clinton v Cedar Rapids and the Missouri River Railroad* has come to be known as Dillon's Rule:

> Municipal corporations owe their origins to, and derive their powers and rights wholly from, the [state] legislature. It breathes into them the breath of life, without which they cannot exist. As it creates, so may it destroy. If it may destroy, it may abridge and control . . . We know of no limitations on this right so far as the [municipal] corporations themselves are concerned. They are, so to phrase it, the mere tenants at will of the legislature (24 Iowa 455; 1868).

Although Dillon's Rule has been widely modified through so-called "home rule" provisions, discussed later in this chapter, it remains the foundational statement of the underlying constitutional relationship between states and local governments in the United States.

As a result, a municipality can take few if any actions to further revitalization that are not directly or potentially subject to state action, whether demolishing a vacant building, selling city property, granting tax exemptions, or requiring developers to provide affordable housing units. The state can give, as when it grants municipalities broad redevelopment powers, or it can take away, as when it limits use of eminent domain or imposes tax and spending caps. State policy can further regional strategies, which can in turn reduce disparities between central cities and their surroundings, but it can also let intermunicipal rivalries and inequities take their course—or even exacerbate them.

Municipalities are not, however, mere passive actors at the mercy of the state. Their success or failure at revitalization is far from a simple function of the policies adopted by their respective states. Local governments always retain the capacity to act, albeit within the framework permitted by state law; even in the most restrictive states, room exists for local initiatives, capacity, and leadership. A city may progress despite poor state policies or fail despite strong, supportive ones. State policies powerfully influence the conduct and outcomes of urban revitalization efforts—but they do not determine them.

The Fiscal Framework

State legal power over local government is reinforced by state control of municipal purse strings. States define which revenue sources local government may tap and under what conditions, set rules that determine how much they can collect in property taxes and from whom, and impose caps on property assessments, tax rates, or annual increases thereof. The procedures that municipalities or counties use to collect delinquent taxes are spelled out by state law down to the finest detail, including the manner in which tax lien auctions are held and the form of the notices that must be given to interested parties. Most states allow municipalities to impose sales taxes, but only 17 allow them to adopt wage or income taxes (Walczak 2019). A few states, including Ohio, allow both. Similarly, all states impose restrictions on municipal borrowing, including the amount of debt they can incur and the purposes for which they may borrow.

As with the power to raise money, states regulate how municipalities can spend it—namely, only for

The City of Dallas, Texas, funded the creation of Klyde Warren Park (opposite) through a public–private partnership that included $20 million each in municipal bond funds and in highway funds from the state, as well as $16.7 million in federal stimulus, to cover its downtown's recessed Woodall Rodgers Freeway. *Source: OJB Landscape Architecture.*

activities the state deems to be public purposes and only under ground rules set by the state. Thus, a Michigan law specifically allows municipalities to spend money on activities such as fireworks for "the proper observance of Armistice, Independence, and Memorial or Decoration Day or . . . a diamond jubilee or centennial" (Michigan Compiled Laws §123.851). While some states have adopted rules governing the form and content of the municipal budget, New Jersey actually requires state approval of individual municipal budgets. While cities generally retain discretion over the details of their own operations and over how to allocate their budgets and personnel among various municipal functions, all of those decisions are made under the state's ultimate authority.

When a local government falls into financial distress or cannot meet debt service or pension obligations, many states step in to exercise varying degrees of control over the municipality. Pennsylvania's Act 47, for example, requires distressed municipalities to prepare remedial action plans under state supervision. In Ohio, the Auditor of State tracks different levels of fiscal distress, from fiscal caution to fiscal emergency, the latter of which triggers state financial supervision (Ohio Revised Code, Chapter 3316). Michigan law similarly allows the state to appoint an emergency manager to take over a city in its entirely, as it did for Detroit in 2013 (MCL 141.1549). At the same time, some other states exercise little or no oversight over municipal finances.

Home Rule, Preemption, and the State–Local Tug-of-War

While Dillon's Rule is the bedrock of the state–local relationship, few states today adhere strictly to it. Other than in Virginia and North Carolina, the rule has been gradually modified to allow varying and even significant levels of municipal discretionary action known as "home rule," often in state constitutions. New Jersey's reads:

The provisions of this Constitution and of any law concerning municipal corporations formed for local government, or concerning counties, shall be liberally construed in their favor. The powers of counties and such municipal corporations shall include not only those granted in express terms but also those of necessary or fair implication, or incident to the powers expressly conferred, or essential thereto, and not inconsistent with or prohibited by this Constitution or by law (N.J. Const. art. 4. sec. 7).

Montana's state constitution similarly but more succinctly reads, "A local government unit adopting a self-government charter may exercise any power not prohibited by this constitution, law, or charter" (Mont. Const. art. 6 sec. 6).

These "home rule" provisions have been adopted by statute in other states, as in the broadly written Florida Home Rule Powers Act:

Under Georgia law, Atlanta was able to create a Tax Allocation District that used tax increment financing to fund the transformative Beltline project. *Source: Christopher T. Martin.*

It is the further intent of the Legislature to extend to municipalities the exercise of powers for municipal governmental, corporate, or proprietary purposes not expressly prohibited by the constitution, general or special law, or county charter and to remove any limitations, judicially imposed or otherwise, on the exercise of home rule powers other than those so expressly prohibited (Fla. Const. art. 8 sec. 2).

In some "hybrid" states, municipalities that meet certain criteria can exercise home rule powers, while others cannot. In Illinois, for instance, any municipality with a population over 25,000 automatically becomes a home rule municipality unless it opts out, while smaller municipalities can become home rule municipalities by local referendum (Il. Const. art. 7 sec. 6).

Under home rule provisions, municipalities can address local concerns and needs under municipal "police power," which allows them to establish and enforce laws protecting public welfare, safety, and health. Thus, the New Jersey Supreme Court has upheld the validity of municipal rent control ordinances, and California municipalities could enact ordinances requiring lenders to maintain properties in foreclosure during the 2007–2008 foreclosure crisis.

The state, however, still ultimately reigns supreme. Home rule provisions do permit municipalities to exercise power, but only in the absence of conflicting state rules. Thus, any local government action can be preempted by state legislative or executive action. If the New Jersey legislature passed a law banning rent control, every local rent control ordinance in effect would cease to have legal force. Legislatures have often exercised this power in recent years, usually in the form of Republican-controlled state legislatures nullifying ordinances enacted by Democratic cities. The Texas legislature nullified an Austin ordinance barring landlords from discriminating against tenants with housing choice vouchers (Texas Local Government Code, Sec. 250.007), and the Missouri legislature reversed a St. Louis minimum wage ordinance (Senate Substitute #2 for HB1193 and 1194, 2017). After the voters of Denton, Texas, banned fracking by referendum, the state legislature passed a law nullifying the referendum and preempting local regulation of oil and gas production (HB 40, 2015). More recently, several governors issued executive orders barring cities from imposing mask-wearing requirements in response to the COVID-19 pandemic.

Home rule and preemption are the two ends of a longstanding tug-of-war between state power and municipal efforts to carve out a sphere of autonomy for themselves. Cities may win the occasional battle, but the states always win the war.

CHAPTER 3
What is Urban Revitalization?

The Pocket Park in Allentown, Pennsylvania, offers a unique outdoor venue for community gatherings and performances along the city's ArtsWalk. *Source: April Gamiz/The Morning Call/TCA.*

Urban revitalization is not an endpoint; rather, it is the sum of many interrelated and ongoing processes in five distinct sectors. As each process unfolds, its effects can either reinforce or undercut changes wrought by the others. The role each sector plays, and how state laws and policies drive or affect them, is discussed in chapters 4 and 5.

- **Strong fiscal capacity and service delivery**: The extent to which the city raises enough funds to provide a robust level of public services to its citizens, businesses, and visitors without imposing an undue tax burden on its residents and properties and to which it has the technical and managerial capacity to provide quality public services and foster revitalization efficiently and effectively

- **A robust real estate market**: The extent to which the city's property market, particularly its housing market and residential neighborhoods, competes successfully within its region and generates sustainable, ongoing investment by property buyers, property owners, and developers

- **A competitive economy**: The extent to which the city provides an environment conducive to economic growth and business success and to which it is competitive within and beyond its region in new business formation, growth of local businesses, and attractiveness to firms moving to the region from elsewhere

- **Healthy neighborhoods and quality of life**: The extent to which the city contains healthy neighborhoods and offers all residents a good quality of life, reflected not only in the quality and affordability of housing and the quality of public services, but also the quality of the physical environment; public safety and public health; and the cultural, artistic, and recreational amenities the community offers

- **Human capital development**: The extent to which the city maximizes its human capital and creates opportunities for good jobs and upward mobility for all its residents through strong educational and workforce development programs and through fostering job and business opportunities

While each of these elements requires separate strategies and investments, they interact with and reinforce one another. Without the economic competitiveness that can enable the city to grow jobs and businesses, or high quality of life that makes the city an attractive place to live and work, a city's ability to

Farmers' markets and other accessible community events can contribute to a city's cultural amenities and enhance quality of life for local residents. *Source: Jamie Bradburn.*

maximize human capital is sharply reduced. In such an environment, successful human capital development may lead not to revitalization but to a "brain drain" as beneficiaries of educational opportunities move elsewhere, seen in many developing countries. Conversely, the absence of a skilled, motivated workforce impedes economic growth.

Similarly, a city's inability to provide adequate public services, or a tax structure that imposes a disproportionate burden on city residents and businesses compared to others in competitive places, puts a city at a disadvantage in building a stronger real estate market or becoming more competitive economically. Indeed, the relationships between them are so strong that if a city fails to make at least some progress in all five elements, that will inevitably handicap its ability to make progress in the others.

How a city goes about pursuing revitalization is less important than its commitment to an intentionally inclusive strategy.

Another issue needs to be part of the equation: inclusion, or the extent to which revitalization benefits all the people of a city, rather than disproportionately benefiting a few. The impacts of recent revivals in older American cities have been uneven at best, with only certain parts of those cities and often small numbers of residents benefiting. Communities of color are rarely among them. Inclusion is not an issue separate from urban revitalization—it is part and parcel of successful efforts.

Inclusion can mean many things and may be reflected in many different policies. At one level, it means a determined effort to ensure at each step that revitalization reaches the entire population and that lower-income neighborhoods and their residents benefit.

That could entail directing new jobs toward underemployed residents, while offering the training and other activities to provide the skills they need for those jobs, or ensuring that a rapidly appreciating neighborhood's future includes affordable housing and avoids displacing residents.

But meaningful inclusion also goes beyond operational steps. Given the racial and ethnic polarization of American cities—and the extent to which that history is rooted in institutionalized power imbalances and abuses—inclusion demands that revitalization recognizes and addresses that history and that people who have been historically excluded from important civic participation actively share in decision-making going forward.

Within these broad parameters, there are many paths to success. How a city goes about pursuing revitalization is less important than its commitment to an intentionally inclusive strategy. For instance, should efforts to develop human capital prioritize improving public education, training workers for specific jobs, or linking educational institutions and employers? While one might answer "all of the above," choices must be made—a city cannot do everything all at once, even under the best of circumstances. The choices, though, should not be random but strategic, driven by realistic yet ambitious goals and based on a coherent theory of change that clearly connects the city's strategies to its goals.

State policies affect all of these choices, and any given body of state policies is likely to impact more than one of the five revitalization elements. While state education policies may drive a city's efforts to develop human capital, the impact of those policies on the city's school system will also affect the quality of a city's neighborhoods and the strength of its housing market. Local education policies that might strengthen human capital might not stabilize neighborhoods or build markets as effectively as other strategies. Policy makers must often make tough choices.

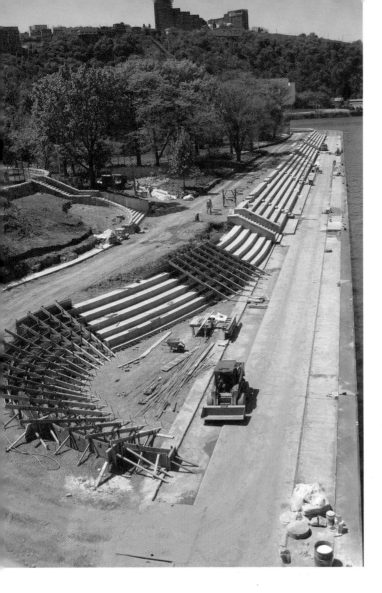

That question surfaces deeply held values about the role of consumer choice in public education—and of public education in general. What constitutes a pro-revitalization or pro-equity policy can ultimately be as normative as it is objective.

The next two chapters drill down into each of the five sectors summarized above, identifying key state policies at work and addressing a few issues related to those policies. They are far from exhaustive; to discuss each state policy in even modest detail would take a lengthy book. While these chapters suggest what may constitute pro-revitalization policies, readers should use those suggestions to think through the question for themselves.

In the final analysis, revitalization is not an outcome. The touchstone of success is not a measurable endpoint but rather sustained improvement over time across all five elements. True equilibrium may be hard to find. In some places, such as San Francisco, California, economic or housing market growth can actually be too successful, to the point that fewer and fewer residents benefit, and more and more are left out. No city can ever rest on its laurels or assume, as many once did, that their economic position was unassailable and that they "had it made." Cities' environments are constantly changing. Revitalization is a never-ending work in progress.

What constitutes a "pro-revitalization" state policy may appear self-evident, but that is not always true. For example, is a state policy pro-revitalization if it prioritizes using Low Income Housing Tax Credits in areas of opportunity with high property values and job growth, rather than in distressed inner-city areas? Answering that question hinges on the assessment of whether such developments improve quality of life in distressed neighborhoods or enhance their housing markets. There is no simple answer.

An area of more vociferous disagreement is whether policies that encourage charter schools or other school-choice alternatives are more or less pro-revitalization or pro-equity than policies that focus on improving the quality of traditional public schools.

CHAPTER 4
State Policies for Economic and Fiscal Revival

Historic theaters serve as anchors for revival in downtown Birmingham, Alabama. *Source: butch_oglesby/Instagram.*

The starting point for any city's revival is its ability to regain economic and fiscal vitality. While that is far from the sum of revival, it is hard to imagine any city's ability to successfully pursue other goals, including equity and opportunity, without a solid economic foundation. A city that struggles to pay its bills, that is hemorrhaging jobs and businesses, and that has homes remaining unsold for lack of demand will be unable to meet the needs of its residents, however good its intentions.

This chapter looks at how states can help cities pursue economic vitality in those three areas: build its fiscal capacity and ability to deliver public services, foster a robust housing market, and stimulate a competitive local economy. In the following chapter we look at the state role in supporting city efforts to create strong neighborhoods and quality of life to maximize the human capital of its residents.

Strengthening Fiscal Capacity and Service Delivery

Cities should have enough revenues to deliver a reasonable quality of public services and public investments without imposing a disproportionate tax burden on residents. While states should set general regional parameters on what constitutes "reasonable," the principles are clear, and municipalities should retain significant flexibility within those parameters. State law governs municipal revenues through three separate bodies of law, policy, and regulation.

MUNICIPAL CAPACITY TO RAISE LOCAL TAX REVENUES

States determine what sources of income or wealth can be taxed by local governments and the rules by which they can be taxed. While the property tax is by far the largest source of local revenue, many states allow some or all municipalities to levy a sales tax, and a smaller number allow some or all municipalities to levy an income or wage tax, which sometimes includes wages earned within the city by workers living outside the city. Most experts agree that tax diversity—raising taxes from a variety of sources rather than relying too heavily on the property tax—stabilizes municipal finance. This appears to be true in Ohio, where state law permits cities to impose income taxes along with sales and property taxes (Wilkinson 2016). Despite cities' individual economic struggles, their fiscal position in Ohio is stronger than that of many peers in more restrictive states.

Whatever local taxes a state government allows, their extent is also defined by state government; all 50 states cap local sales and income tax rates. Absolute caps on property taxes such as California's Proposition 13 may be best known, but other

A popular destination since the 1860s, Market Square in Knoxville, Tennessee, is home to a variety of local businesses.
Source: David Wilson/Flickr.

limitations are more common, including widespread limitations on annual increases. While the state may reasonably establish some constraints on municipal taxation, as seen in table 4.1, many limitations— which typically apply across the board to all municipalities in the state—in practice unreasonably constrain cities' ability to provide adequate municipal services and invest in their futures. Property tax caps also tend to be regressive, creating inequities among jurisdictions and between longtime owners and recent homebuyers (Fiscal Policy Institute 2015). High property tax rates can push down property values and discourage investment, but it's a devil's bargain to force municipalities to keep taxes low if it impedes their ability to provide decent public services for residents and businesses.

Table 4.1

State Policies Affecting Fiscal Capacity and Service Delivery

Category	State Policy Description	Pro-Revitalization Features
Local Revenue Sources	Defines municipal ability to use multiple revenue sources, including local property taxes, income or wage taxes, sales taxes, and other taxes and user charges.	Greater flexibility allows a municipality to utilize multiple revenue sources.
Level of Local Revenue Sources	Limits local revenue sources, such as with caps on property tax rates or annual increases.	Sufficiently flexible or nonexistent caps allow municipalities to address both service delivery and investment needs.
Property Tax Assessment	Governs how property taxes are assessed.	Municipal authority to establish tax classification categories within clear state guidelines, and to vary tax rates on land and improvement, permits use of tax policy to further revitalization goals.
Level of and Terms Governing State Aid to Local Governments	Defines the extent to which states provide aid to supplement municipal own-revenue sources and the terms governing that aid.	Need-based municipal aid can meaningfully redress fiscal imbalances and inequity, especially where conditions for providing aid do not unreasonably impair municipal investment and service delivery.
Ability of Municipalities to Obtain Host Benefits	Defines the extent to which states permit municipalities to obtain reasonable financial benefit from specialized or non-taxable facilities, including casinos, hospitals, and governmental facilities.	PILOTs from tax-exempt facilities, and fair allocation of tax revenues from local facilities such as casinos, enable municipalities to cover costs and derive fiscal benefits from location of specialized or tax-exempt facilities.
Rules Governing Municipal Spending and Service Delivery	Constrains or mandates municipal spending, such as by imposing work rules.	Flexible laws governing municipal spending within broad criteria and avoidance of state mandates dictating terms and conditions of local service delivery and investment can maximize local ability to focus on revitalization.
Rules Governing Fiscal Transparency and Oversight of Municipal Finances	Monitors municipal budgets and financial practices and dictates when and how the state may intervene to address municipal fiscal issues and problems.	High level of local fiscal transparency, strong reporting requirements, and professional state oversight can add up to a well-designed system that permits state intervention to help municipalities solve fiscal problems, with state control as last resort when fiscal problems overwhelm local capacity.

MUNICIPAL ABILITY TO IMPOSE FEES AND USER CHARGES

Fees and user charges account for nearly a quarter of all local general revenues. Fees often cover the cost of providing water and sewerage service but can also include airport, parking, and development impact fees, among others. State laws govern what is considered a fee versus a tax, where municipalities can impose fees, how much they can charge, and how they can use the fees collected. For example, a Massachusetts law, since repealed, limited the fee Boston could charge to tow illegally parked cars to just $12, far less than the city's cost (Frug and Barron 2008).

While many fees may be equity-neutral, in that they do not inordinately burden some classes of residents or businesses (particularly lower-income residents), some pose troubling issues. Missouri law restricts nearly all forms of municipal taxation except fines and fees, which has led some small municipalities to effectively turn their police departments and courts into money machines preying on Black and lower-income people. Writing for *Slate*, reporter Reihan Salam described "towns too small or too starved of sales tax revenues to sustain their own local governments [that] stay afloat by having local law enforcement go trawling for trumped-up traffic violations, the fines for which can be cripplingly expensive, and which only grow more onerous as low-income residents fail to pay them" (2014). This points out a larger issue in the state–local fiscal relationship: While states may allocate public resources inequitably in some cases, state laws may be needed to curb inequitable practices by *local* government in others.

STATE AID TO LOCAL GOVERNMENTS

Transfer payments make up nearly one-third of all local general revenues. Nearly 90 percent of those payments come from state government, including federal funds passed through the state. State aid to local governments has declined in many states over the past decade, however, and despite widespread fiscal recovery at the state level, cuts made during the Great Recession between 2007 and 2009 have largely not been restored. Since both property values and incomes are usually lower in older cities than in suburbs, state aid is critical to cities' ability to attain fiscal stability and deliver services reliably. State aid to municipalities varies widely; state aid in Connecticut and Maryland accounts for more than 30 percent of municipal budgets, whereas Georgia and Oklahoma provide 3 percent or less (McFarland and Hoene 2015). Conditions on state aid are also important; New Jersey uses much-needed supplemental state aid for distressed cities as a lever to impose sometimes appropriate but often severe conditions on municipal beneficiaries.

While states may allocate public resources inequitably in some cases, state laws may be needed to curb inequitable practices by local government in others.

The fiscal relationship between states and cities is complex and often marred by suspicion or outright conflict. When cities desperately need state aid, it can foster a culture of dependency as well as high-handedness by the state. While cities may resent state patronage, it may often be needed, though limited resources are seldom the sole cause of fiscal problems or poor service delivery. A study of Pennsylvania's Act 47 program of aid to distressed cities found that "Pennsylvania's cities . . . contribute to their own distress through mismanagement, political infighting, and poor financial judgment" (Fehr 2012).

It is a difficult balancing act. Too much state control over municipal finances means that service delivery, innovation, and creativity are stifled. Too little, and mismanagement or corruption can follow. The problem of "regulatory stringency with low expectations" is that states often take for granted that municipalities are incompetent or corrupt, and thus they offer no incentives to encourage local officials to proactively

The City of Baltimore, Maryland, has made substantial reinvestments in East Baltimore in recent years, including in housing and connective corridors. *Source: Anne Ditmeyer/ Prêt à Voyager/Flickr.*

or creatively solve problems (Mallach and Sterner 2008). On the contrary, cities often find that any deviation from tried-and-true practice is greeted with hostility by state regulators, and local officials then find themselves going to great lengths to bend state rules in order to pursue the activities needed to further local goals.

These issues underlie the dynamics of the state–local fiscal relationship. Some level of state oversight of municipal finances is appropriate and desirable. Too much, and it becomes a burden. The challenge is to calibrate state oversight to actively incentivize effective local governance, service delivery, and creative revital- ization strategies, rather than accepting mediocrity as the norm or focusing on sanctions for bad behavior.

Fostering a Robust Housing Market

In most cities, the majority of land is residential and makes up the greater part of the city's property value and tax base. Building demand for a city as a place to live is essential to revitalization; indeed, no city can revive unless people want to live in it and are willing to pay reasonable prices for its housing stock. By reasonable, we do not mean the superheated prices of Washington, DC, or New York City—but high enough that owners are motivated to improve their properties and developers are motivated to rehabilitate vacant buildings or lots. For that to happen, prices must equal or exceed the replacement costs of existing housing stock; areas where prices are lower and where the costs to acquire and rehabilitate a building are greater than its market value are referred to as having a "market gap."

Successful economic development affects a city's housing market, but those effects are often both limited and uneven. If the people who fill new jobs live in the suburbs, job growth will have little impact on in-city housing markets. Conversely, if economic development results in significant numbers of existing community residents getting better jobs, that may have positive spillover effects on housing markets in their neighborhoods. Otherwise, economic development spillovers most often affect only those areas that already have the greatest market potential—in and around downtowns, by major universities and medical centers, or in areas with special attributes such as waterfronts or historic buildings. For a city to realize broad, sustained improvement in housing market conditions across the city, it must pursue intentional strategies toward that end.

States influence the ability of local governments and of key nongovernmental actors such as community development corporations (CDCs) to mount such strategies in two major respects:

- the state legal framework governing the regulatory tools and reuse options that a municipality can deploy to address problem property issues; and
- the state's provision of targeted resources and incentives to facilitate market-building, either directly or through broader neighborhood revitalization programs.

TOOLS FOR REGULATING AND REUSING PROBLEM PROPERTIES

Neighborhoods with weak housing markets and low property values typically contain many problem properties, including vacant abandoned structures and substandard, ill-maintained, absentee-owned rental buildings. Problem properties exacerbate neighborhood problems, depressing property values and increasing crime, itself a major factor in depressing demand. Programs by which local governments can compel owners to improve problem properties, take them from recalcitrant or absent owners and place them in responsible hands for reuse, or demolish them, are all critical to any neighborhood market-building strategy.

For a city to realize broad, sustained improvement in housing market conditions across the city, it must pursue intentional strategies toward that end.

Over many years, numerous tools have emerged to regulate and reuse problem property, but cities across the United States utilize them to widely varying degrees. They include:

- **code enforcement**, requiring owners to maintain property in keeping with state or local maintenance requirements, health standards, and other policies;
- **vacant property registration**, requiring owners of vacant properties to register with the city, pay fees reflecting the city's costs to deal with vacant properties, and maintain and secure their properties;
- **vacant property receivership**, under which municipalities or nongovernmental actors can gain control of vacant properties through court proceedings to restore them to use;
- **vacant property acquisition tools**, including provisions for accelerated tax foreclosure of vacant properties and for forfeiture and spot blight eminent domain statutes, which allow municipalities to take individual blighted properties and convey them to responsible owners for reuse;
- **land banking**, the ability to create dedicated entities with power to obtain properties through tax foreclosure and otherwise and position them for productive reuse;

- **lender responsibility tools,** holding lenders responsible for maintaining vacant properties during foreclosure proceedings pending change of title; and

- **rental licensing,** requiring owners of rental housing to maintain properties according to reasonable standards in order to obtain a license permitting them to rent the property.

What local governments can do in all of these areas is largely driven by state law, which varies widely with respect to the freedom of action allowed municipalities, as shown in table 4.2. In states that adhere strictly to Dillon's Rule, municipalities can regulate properties only within the explicit bounds set by state statutes. Elsewhere, however, home-rule language allows local governments flexibility through use of the police power.

Table 4.2

Policies Affecting Housing Markets

Category	State Policy Description	Pro-Revitalization Features
Market-building Incentives	Build stronger markets in weak-market areas with tax credits, other assistance for neighborhood investment, or incentives for mixed-income or mixed-use development.	State policies that provide incentives for market-rate housing stabilize or revitalize neighborhoods where market-building is needed.
Affordable Housing Location Policies	Guide the distribution of affordable housing resources by location, such as the state's Qualified Allocation Plan, fair share plans, and inclusionary housing regulations.	A balanced distribution of affordable housing resources between different community types encourages mobility of lower-income households, rather than concentrating poverty and affordable housing in low-income urban neighborhoods.
Financing Tools	Increase access to mortgage financing and other forms of real estate development financing.	Facilitating home buying in urban areas, rehabilitation, and new construction—and increasing mortgage access for lower-income households unable to obtain conventional financing—can stabilize and improve housing markets.
Land Use Regulation	Govern municipal land use regulatory authority, as well as larger state and regional planning laws that affect local land use planning.	Flexible and strong tools allow municipalities to regulate development while setting clear limits on exclusionary land use practices.
Property Regulation Tools	Govern code enforcement, rental housing regulation, and vacant property regulation.	Flexible and strong tools allow municipalities to regulate problem properties.
Property Acquisition Tools	Govern acquisition of property by public entities, including land banking, receivership, and eminent domain.	Flexible and strong tools allow municipalities to gain control of problem properties, through land banking, receivership, and other means.
Support For Community Development and Neighborhood Revitalization	Address broader, multifaceted community development and neighborhood revitalization activities, over and above programs that address specific revitalization issues such as housing or code enforcement.	Programs that support multifaceted community development and neighborhood revitalization programs encourage comprehensive equitable revitalization strategies and provide support for activities for which dedicated funding is unavailable.

Federal tax credits, a state grant, foundation funding, and developer equity all came together to make possible Marketplace Apartments, a mixed-income rental development in downtown Flint, Michigan. *Source: Michael Gleason Photography.*

That flexibility exists only where state law is silent, however; it is unlikely a court would uphold a municipal spot blight eminent domain ordinance that was not explicitly permitted by state law, for instance, as all states have statutes regulating the use of eminent domain. Cities in a number of states, however, have successfully used the police power to adopt vacant property registration ordinances, since no state law existed to address those issues one way or another. Although only four states have adopted statutes governing vacant property registration (Georgia, Nebraska, Virginia, and West Virginia), nearly 1,700 municipalities across the country have adopted such ordinances, including large numbers in New Jersey, New York, and Pennsylvania.

State-by-state variation extends to the minutiae of these statutes. Illinois permits nongovernmental entities to pursue receivership actions against problem properties, but New Jersey gives standing only to municipal governments. Virginia allows licensing of rental housing—but only in designated "rental inspection districts." In Illinois, home-rule cities may adopt rental licensing ordinances, but non–home-rule cities may not. Similar variations can be cited ad infinitum.

As a result, the manner in which cities can exercise regulatory power to deal with problem properties is a patchwork. Some states may permit vacant property receivership but not spot blight eminent domain, while others may permit the latter but not the former.

Each city must navigate its particular path through the opportunities offered and constraints imposed by the state.

TARGETED RESOURCES AND INCENTIVES

Strengthening housing markets in disinvested areas where property values are low and where a market gap exists almost always requires initial public sector investment. Though market potential may exist, developers and investors are unlikely to put money into distressed, low-value areas without public sector assistance to jump-start the market. While many struggling cities and towns want to build stronger markets—citywide or in targeted neighborhoods— few have adequate local resources available.

Strategies for creating stronger housing markets are very different from those for creating housing to meet affordability needs. Affordable housing is designed to be for households below certain income levels, priced to rent or sell at levels those households can afford, and meant primarily to improve the quality of residents' lives. It operates outside the market, and its effects on housing markets thus vary widely. While a well-designed affordable housing project may in some cases have a positive market effect by helping to stabilize a block or a neighborhood, it may have a negative effect in others, potentially undermining the private, unsubsidized market.

States can facilitate local market-building activities in a number of ways, such as:

- authorizing municipalities to incentivize market-building activities, including granting tax abatements;

- providing financial incentives to fill market gaps in areas where the city or other entities seek to build stronger markets; and

- increasing access to capital for home buyers and developers in emerging market areas.

As cities rarely have adequate discretionary funds to fill market gaps directly, they most often use tax abatements to incentivize markets, under which a project will make payments equal to only a small part of the property taxes they would otherwise be required to pay, for some period, typically between five and thirty years. Some states permit municipalities to offer such abatements only in specific, explicit ways, while others allow broad flexibility to craft targeted tax abatements.

While tax abatements in various forms have been around for many decades, a number of states have in recent years adopted other types of market-building incentives. Oregon's Vertical Housing Program, first enacted in 2001, offers special tax benefits for

---

Since 1995, the state of Delaware has spent over $370 million to develop Riverfront Wilmington, an abandoned industrial area now transformed into a major hub of business, entertainment, and residential life. *Source: likeaduck/Flickr.*

mixed-use, multistory, multifamily housing in designated "Vertical Housing Zones." From 1996 to 2014, the New Jersey Housing and Mortgage Agency's CHOICE program (Choices in Home Ownership Incentives Created for Everyone) provided construction financing and gap subsidies for developers building housing for home ownership in targeted areas.

Rarely do state laws explicitly bar municipalities from pursuing market-building activities as a matter of law, but states should go further to help distressed cities build stronger housing markets. As limited financial resources can effectively make it impossible for municipalities to pursue strategies with significant revitalization potential, their state's readiness to provide financial resources to support local strategies can determine the success or failure of a market-building strategy.

While market building can benefit all residents of a community, it does not automatically do so. State assistance should be governed by rules that ensure lower-income residents of targeted neighborhoods benefit accordingly. One way to do that is through inclusionary zoning—that is, mandating a percentage of new housing units be affordable for low- and moderate-income households. While some states have done that, others have taken the opposite course and passed laws prohibiting municipalities from enacting inclusionary ordinances, either as a result of pressure from developers or hostility to what they consider a form of rent control or social engineering.

Stimulating a Competitive Economy

A recurrent theme among America's older cities over the past half-century is the ongoing search for new economic engines to replace those lost with the decline of urban manufacturing. The most successful cities have capitalized on their unique assets, particularly major educational and medical facilities like Johns Hopkins University in Baltimore, Maryland, or the University of Pennsylvania in Philadelphia, which are each their city's largest employer. Historic and locational assets have also enabled cities to build economic engines based on entertainment and tourism and to draw thousands of highly skilled young college graduates, who bring both talent and spending. Without explicit strategies to distribute the gains from these new economic engines, however, the benefits tend to be narrowly concentrated, leaving out most of a city and its residents. How to harness the awesome economic power of major educational and medical institutions for equitable, inclusive economic growth, then, is a major challenge facing local governments—and one where the state laws governing those institutions have a major effect.

A recurrent theme among America's older cities over the past half-century is the ongoing search for new economic engines to replace those lost with the decline of urban manufacturing.

States rarely drive specific local economic development efforts directly, although there are exceptions; under Governor Ed Rendell, Pennsylvania provided $100 million to the City of Scranton in 2009 to further downtown revitalization by creating a new medical school, and the state of Delaware has led Wilmington's Riverfront redevelopment since the mid-1990s. State government, however, consistently plays a major role in setting the rules that govern municipal economic development, strongly influencing the extent to which a city can capitalize on its assets and equitably direct the resulting benefits to its citizens at large. Two areas where the state plays such a role are economic incentives and redevelopment tools. Both are not only important but also raise highly contested policy issues.

ECONOMIC INCENTIVES

Most if not all states offer incentives to promote development and attract businesses, such as tax credits and abatements, provision of building sites and worker training, direct financial support through grants or loans, and others described in table 4.3. Many of these incentives are provided on a case-by-case basis, though some operate through versions of enterprise zones in which all businesses in a defined geographic area are eligible for benefits. Many states have also subsidized the cost of convention centers, arenas, and stadiums.

The evidence for the value of these incentives is mixed. Peters and Fisher's survey of economic incentives concluded that they "produce an unending merry-go-round of tax cuts and subsidies whose net effect is to starve government of the resources it needs to finance the services it should be providing and to make the state and local tax system ever more regressive" (Peters and Fisher 2004). Others argue that, despite abuses, incentives can play a valuable role in spurring economic growth and providing community benefits. They suggest that incentives can be designed to benefit targeted areas and their residents, rather than simply enrich already-prosperous corporations (Bardik 2019).

The construction of Camden Tower, a 375,000-square-foot office complex on the Camden, New Jersey, waterfront (opposite), was made possible thanks to $245 million in New Jersey state tax incentives. *Source: Philly by Drone.*

Table 4.3

Policies Affecting Economic Competitiveness

Category	State Policy Description	Pro-Revitalization Features
Economic Incentives	Promote business growth, business relocation, and job creation through tax credits, grants, and other assistance.	Transparent incentives provide for urban and need-based targeting and may be applied on the basis of clear need and community benefit criteria.
Financing Programs	Provide short- and long-term loan capital to businesses for property acquisition, fit-out and start-up costs, inventory, or other small business needs.	Real estate-based and business-based loan programs that are accessible to small and large businesses can improve access to capital in capital-deprived areas and enhance neighborhood revitalization and redevelopment programs.
Redevelopment Tools	Provide local governments with legal and fiscal capabilities for redevelopment, including eminent domain, tax increment financing, and revenue bond issuance.	Broad legal authority for local governments to apply redevelopment tools, with clear ground rules to ensure their proper and transparent use, can maximize redevelopment capability while minimizing abuses.
Transportation Programs	Provide for construction of new road and transit programs, repair and upgrading of existing facilities, and operating support for transit and road maintenance, including improvements for pedestrians and cyclists.	Policies based on municipal need can favor capital and operating support for transit systems, upgrades to existing roads and highways, and increased walking and biking opportunities, rather than new highway construction.
Regional Frameworks	Govern economic development at the regional level.	Coordinated economic development strategies and programs within metro areas can further a clear focus on the needs of urban areas and increase the potential for inclusive revitalization.

From a revitalization perspective, state urban economic incentives should meet three paramount criteria:

1. Incentives should target areas of need rather than being location-neutral.

2. Incentive criteria should include meaningful benefits for community residents, particularly lower-income residents and people of color.

3. Benefits realized by the incentive should exceed opportunity costs; that is, they should exceed those benefits to the public good that could have been realized for the same public expenditure if used for some other public purpose.

New Jersey's Grow NJ program vividly exemplifies some of the pitfalls of incentives that fail to meet these criteria. New Jersey's program targets distressed areas, and the most generous incentives are available in the state's four poorest cities. From late 2013 through 2015, the state allocated $1.1 billion in tax incentives under this program to 16 projects in the city of Camden (Nurin 2015).

Camden is deeply distressed—by many measures, it is one of the poorest cities in America—but the benefits derived from this vast expenditure proved highly questionable at best. In most cases, companies were paid to relocate existing workers from facilities in nearby suburbs, while promising to create a small number of new jobs. The average incentive payment per job over a 10-year period is nearly $400,000, with no assurance that any of the existing workers will move to Camden or that any of the new jobs would be filled by Camden residents. The benefits to Camden's residents are thus minimal; from the perspective of opportunity costs, the state resources forgone to pay for these incentives could have been used in ways that would have created far greater benefits for the city and for its lower-income residents.

Four straightforward criteria should govern truly pro-revitalization incentives:

1. Ensure that there are significant and tangible community job and other benefits.

2. Link incentives to training programs and "first source" agreements that require employers to give preference to qualified local residents to maximize local hiring.

3. Conduct rigorous cost-benefit and "but for" assessments.

4. Build in "clawbacks" for recapture and potential disqualification from future incentives if the company's performance does not match the conditions of the incentive.

These are not complex criteria. The challenges to crafting equitable, pro-revitalization incentives are arguably more political than technical—which may contribute to the tendency of many commentators to condemn the entire practice out of hand.

REDEVELOPMENT TOOLS

In contrast to outer suburbs with greenfield sites yet to be developed, older cities must redevelop currently or formerly used land and buildings to accommodate future economic growth. This can be a daunting challenge: Redevelopment can trigger high costs for land acquisition, site assembly, environmental remediation, and demolition—not to mention potentially ruinous delays at any step, placing urban sites at a competitive disadvantage to their suburban neighbors.

Older cities like Chelsea, Massachusetts, must consider particular challenges when redeveloping brownfield sites like the former Forbes Lithographic Company property. *Source: Massachusetts Department of Environmental Protection/Flickr.*

To address these competitive barriers, states have provided cities with a menu of what are collectively called "redevelopment tools," legal and financial mechanisms designed to reduce disparities between urban and suburban development and to render themselves more competitive for private investment. The country's first large-scale redevelopment program, the Urban Renewal program created by the Housing Act of 1949, was driven by a set of erroneous assumptions about what cities needed to be competitive, which led to the widespread destruction of urban

neighborhoods and communities of color. In contrast, today's redevelopment toolkit, rather than prescribing one path to revitalization, can be used in different ways by local governments.

Municipalities have no inherent redevelopment powers, but they depend on widely varying state laws, which allow them, to varying degrees, to:

- carry out redevelopment activities and partner with private entities;
- issue mortgage and industrial revenue bonds (MRBs and IRBs);
- use eminent domain to take property for redevelopment or economic development;
- use tax increment financing (TIF) and create TIF districts;
- create special taxing and improvement districts; and
- grant local tax abatements.

While specific powers can be used in different ways, which may or may not further equitable revitalization, these powers can be part of the essential framework for pursuing revitalization. States that provide cities with the greatest flexibility to use these tools, while maintaining reasonable oversight over their use, can be seen as most pro-revitalization. Despite some cities' limited capacity, states are rarely in a better position than a city itself to determine what an economic development strategy should be or how to implement it. How state laws are drafted and administered, however, can have a powerful bearing on whether their use leads to equity and revitalization.

Governor Rendell's Community Assistance Team (CAT) program in Pennsylvania established in 2004 was a thoughtful approach to supporting local redevelopment. CAT's mission was first to provide technical assistance to cities in developing major local economic development initiatives. Once the city had developed a project that CAT staff had successfully vetted, the team coordinated the state agencies needed to make the project a reality.

How state laws are drafted and administered can have a powerful bearing on whether their use leads to equity and revitalization.

All these redevelopment tools may be needed to draw investment to distressed towns and cities; they are closely related and complement one another. The ability to designate redevelopment areas is far more powerful if linked to the ability to use eminent domain, issue tax abatements, or create TIF districts. Indeed, in some cases, all of these tools may be needed to level the playing field for those involved in urban redevelopment. If some municipalities are given too much latitude in using these tools without adequate state oversight, however, they may be abused.

Eminent domain is a case in point. Most states had flexible eminent domain laws until 2005, when the Supreme Court's 2005 *Kelo v. New London* decision upheld a highly questionable municipal action that was nonetheless well rooted in established legal doctrine. The backlash against that decision led many states to pass laws severely restricting its use. While some of those restrictions were reasonable, others created significant impediments to legitimate redevelopment activities. In Michigan, for example, a ban on eminent domain for economic development projects meant that speculators in Detroit could block critical redevelopment projects by buying strategic vacant land parcels, forcing the city to either pay exorbitant prices for their land or forgo the project.

Similarly, while TIF and tax abatements are valuable redevelopment tools, they also potentially divert or remove revenues that would otherwise have been available for municipal service provision. This places a high burden on local governments to ensure not only that a tool is needed but also that it will ultimately benefit the community's residents. While both mechanisms are grounded in the principle that the development would not have happened but for the incentive (the "but for" test), there is no simple mathematical formula to prove it, and many states and cities fail to do the level of analysis needed to establish it with any confidence.

Much of the local abuse of state-authorized redevelopment tools is due to their lack of transparency, which states rarely address. All such matters—like the criteria used to determine whether a property may be taken through eminent domain, the basis for setting sales prices for properties in redevelopment areas, or whether need exists for tax abatements—should be subject to strong, explicit procedural and disclosure standards. That is a far better way to prevent abuse than either abolishing redevelopment tools or imposing burdensome state oversight, which cripples municipal creativity.

For the most part, these tools are on their face neutral with respect to equity and inclusion, but that does not mean that their outcomes are necessarily neutral. As we have pointed out, seemingly neutral policies can perpetuate and exacerbate an inequitable status quo. As with economic incentives, state statutes governing redevelopment need to include provisions that ensure their use by local governments furthers inclusion and does not exacerbate existing inequities.

Texas laws authorizing tax increment financing made Houston's $324 million public light rail transit system, MetroRail, a viable project. *Source: Marco Moerland/Flickr.*

CHAPTER 5
State Policies for Opportunity and Stronger Communities

A city's economic vitality is not an end in itself but rather a means by which a city can provide a better quality of life for all of its residents and offer them the opportunity to leverage the full measure of their talents and abilities. How well a city realizes those goals is reflected by the quality of the city's neighborhoods and the extent to which every resident can build their own human capital and participate fully in the local economy through the city's educational and workforce development systems.

Visitors to the Springfield Old Capitol Art Fair in Illinois's capital city admire local artists' work. *Source: Illinois Times.*

Cultivating Healthy Neighborhoods and Quality of Life

The preceding sections focused on strategies addressing cities' fiscal and economic bottom lines, which are often seen as the fundamental building blocks of revitalization. Other important factors include the quality of life a city offers to its residents; the quality of its neighborhoods; its public realm of streets, sidewalks, shade trees, and public spaces; and its artistic and cultural climate. This is particularly true today. The move from industry to what has been called the "knowledge sector" and young workers' shifting preferences have led to conditions in which a community's quality of life enhances its economic competitiveness (Clark 2011; Florida 2002). Moreover, the same densely populated, vital mixed-use neighborhoods that have drawn a generation of educated millennials to cities are likely to work for many other people, making the city more attractive to existing residents as well as to other potential newcomers.

While state regulation plays a limited overt role in driving or constraining cities' efforts to build healthier neighborhoods and improve conditions for residents, state laws do have subtle but powerful effects on municipal efforts to enhance quality of life. These extend to many seemingly routine operating responsibilities of city government—most notably through the state role in defining local police activities.

As policing has become an increasingly urgent issue, particularly in Black and Brown communities, the importance of the state's role in creating some of the problems faced by those communities has become far more apparent. State laws actually or potentially control every aspect of local police department behavior, from whether chokeholds may be used to whether disciplinary proceedings become matters of public record. Until its repeal in 2020, Section 50-a of the New York State Civil Rights Law permitted law enforcement officers to refuse disclosing personnel records used to evaluate performance toward continued employment or promotion, effectively preventing outside oversight of police behavior.

A number of states have adopted statutes, sometimes called "police chiefs' bills of rights," that limit the power of local elected leaders to set policy for police departments. Under New Jersey law, a mayor who

Community gardens, such as this one in Newark, New Jersey, have become a common way for urban residents to reutilize vacant land for community benefit. *Source: Yellow Dog Productions/ DigitalVisions/Getty Images.*

wanted to institute community-based foot patrols, for example, could be overruled by the police chief, who by statute has the sole authority to "prescribe the duties and assignments of all subordinates and other personnel." States should repeal statutes that block policing reform and take affirmative steps to support reform, including mandating more extensive officer training and allowing municipal governments to design creative ways to reform or restructure police departments to meet community needs.

Similarly, how the state allocates housing resources such as Low Income Housing Tax Credits—and the extent to which allocation accounts for neighborhood revitalization goals—can help determine success or failure of particular strategies. Indeed, the complexities of siting subsidized housing projects and their uneven effects on a neighborhood point to the complex relationship between equity objectives and a city's neighborhood strategies, given limited resources. Should affordable housing funds, for example, target neighborhoods that are seeing property values rise in order to enable residents to remain? Should those funds be used to improve housing conditions in more distressed neighborhoods? Or should they focus on enabling lower-income residents and people of color to move to suburban areas of opportunity?

The principal role state policy plays in enhancing the physical environment of neighborhoods lies in the allocation of resources, as expanded upon in table 5.1.

Table 5.1

Policies Affecting Healthy Neighborhoods and Quality of Life

Category	State Policy Description	Pro-Revitalization Features
Public Open Space and Vacant Land	Create and maintain public open space and recreational facilities and support maintenance and green uses of vacant urban land, including green infrastructure to address combined sewerage system overflows.	Policies that support quality urban parks and recreational facilities encourage creative green reuse of vacant urban land.
Affordable Housing	Finance construction and rehabilitation of housing for low-income households (means-tested).	Policies that locate housing in areas of opportunity and/or tied to comprehensive neighborhood improvement strategies can foster equitable development and increase opportunities for lower-income families.
Historic Preservation	Govern reuse of historic properties, including tax credits for owners and rehabbers, and for creating and improving historic districts and Main Streets.	Targeted incentives for home buyers and developers to reuse historic properties can overcome market gaps, with clear standards for using historic districts as a revitalization tool.
Neighborhood Revitalization	Address and support the full range of multifaceted neighborhood revitalization activities, rather than limiting engagement to narrowly defined revitalization elements such as housing or code enforcement.	Programs that support multifaceted and equitable neighborhood revitalization encourage comprehensive strategies and support activities for which dedicated funding is unavailable.
Arts and Culture	Support and enable artistic and cultural activities, including public arts programs, artists' housing, and placemaking.	Linking arts, culture, and placemaking to urban revitalization and economic development strategies can enhance the impacts and benefits of neighborhood revitalization activities.

Cities rarely have the fiscal capacity to invest fully in stronger neighborhoods or enhanced quality of life; local governments have also had to drastically cut back parks and recreation personnel over the past few decades and have few resources to create or restore parks. Instead of the necessary sustained engagement, state governments typically provide only limited, intermittent support or funding for activities designed to bring about neighborhood change. An example of a one-shot initiative is California's State Urban Parks and Health Communities program. In a 2002 bond issue, California voters authorized a modest $23.5 million for this program—and by 2006, these funds had been spent and were never replenished.

Few state governments appear to understand the important role they can and should play in helping distressed cities build healthy neighborhoods and improve their quality of life.

Many states offer tax credits for activities that can support healthy neighborhoods; in fact, 30 offer historic preservation tax credits, including for income-producing projects, which can be used to leverage federal historic preservation tax credits and allow individual homeowners to restore their homes. Missouri's enactment of a historic preservation tax credit in 2000 enabled developers to leverage the federal tax credit and helped catalyze the revitalization of the Washington Avenue area of St. Louis, today a prime residential area for millennials and a major entertainment destination. Indeed, one way for a state to generate powerful positive investment outcomes with modest tax expenditures is by enacting state tax credits that leverage existing federal ones, and a number of states have created such "piggyback" credits to leverage the federal Low Income Housing Tax Credit (LIHTC) program.

A more problematic approach to piggybacking can be seen in the state policy response to the federal Opportunity Zone (OZ) program in 2018. The federal law provides powerful financial rewards for investment in distressed lower-income communities, but it lacks safeguards or internal incentives to discourage gentrification or displacement or to ensure that OZ investments go to projects that would not have seen investment but for the incentive. States do have the legal authority to use incentives for OZ investments to foster more equitable outcomes, but only Maryland appears to have done so. Many more, eager to get investment of any kind, have offered state incentives to sweeten the pot for investors of all kinds, without considering how their actions will affect equity.

Many state tax credit programs are also limited by annual caps on the total amount of credits that can be issued. Connecticut caps its historic tax credit for owner-occupied properties at $3 million per year, while Kentucky caps the total tax credit for both residential and income-producing properties at $5 million per year. Spread across an entire state—and not targeted to areas in need of revitalization—these programs have little impact on neighborhood revival.

Some states provide tax credits for neighborhood revitalization. The first of its kind, Pennsylvania's Neighborhood Assistance Program (NAP) was created in 1967 to offer ways for businesses to obtain tax credits by contributing to neighborhood revitalization programs. Through NAP, firms can get a 55 percent tax credit by making a single contribution to support a project in a distressed neighborhood; the project can be in any one of eight categories, which include economic development, affordable housing, crime prevention, and education. Under the Neighborhood Partnership Program, added in 2007, a firm can obtain a tax credit up to 80 percent by entering into a partnership of no less than five years with a community-based nonprofit organization. Similar programs exist in New Jersey, Massachusetts, and other states; while valuable,

their scale is nonetheless modest, and their effects likely to be more ameliorative than transformative.

In the final analysis, few state governments appear to understand the important role they can and should play in helping distressed cities build healthy neighborhoods and improve their quality of life, notwithstanding powerful evidence that suggests such activities may be as or more important to urban revitalization than conventional economic development strategies. The lack of state interest in this area may reflect many different things. On the one hand, neighborhood programs are much less clearly defined and specific than housing projects—or the sort of economic incentive designed to attract a specific business venture. On the other hand, issues of race and class equity may play a role here, too, as the neighborhoods in greatest need of assistance to further their rebuilding are likely to be low-income communities, which are disproportionately communities of color.

The Rise Up Festival in St. Louis, Missouri, celebrates the city's revitalization with an emphasis on local music, art, and food in the Washington Avenue neighborhood. *Source: Larry Perlmutter/Rise Community Development.*

Building Human Capital

The ability of individuals to develop their human capital—that is, obtain an education, gain skills and expertise, and obtain jobs or develop business opportunities from early childhood through adulthood—drives sustainable revitalization by providing the skilled individuals needed to fuel a growing economy. Opportunity to build their human capital also determines how much those individuals will be able to benefit from the economic opportunities created through revitalization. The opportunities a city or region offers its lower-income and minority residents to develop their human capital also largely determines the inclusivity of a city's revitalization, in the sense that benefits will or will not reach the community as a whole.

Given the constant change in the skills the American economy demands of its workforce, human capital development it is not a "one and done" process that ends with the individual gaining stable employment. Rather, it is an ongoing, lifelong process of learning and adaptation, shown in table 5.2, that is important in itself and the critical element through which inclusivity can be best integrated into the revitalization process. Sustainable economic development requires access to a workforce that is both large enough and skilled enough to support economic growth, and that

The Washington State Department of Transportation completed construction on the nearly 1.5-mile SR 520 Floating Bridge and Landings Project in 2016, connecting Seattle and Medina across Lake Washington. *Source: Washington State Department of Transportation/Flickr.*

workforce may be drawn from many different places. At present, though, job growth in revitalizing cities is largely fueled by a suburban workforce, rather than the city's own residents.

In a typical urban area, human capital develops through a plethora of public, private, and nonprofit entities, often poorly coordinated with one another. As a result, a key challenge becomes the sheer number of different, highly fragmented entities and programs that provide these services in lieu of one seamless process that enables individuals to progress steadily toward their goals. Even where all the needed services do exist, the burden is still on the individual (or their parents) to navigate the system and take advantage of those resources. The fragmentation of services and their failure to target those most in need or to adapt to individual needs and conditions means that vast public sums are spent without commensurate benefit (Andreason and Carpenter 2015).

Throughout these systems, state government plays a powerful role in setting policy, adopting and

Table 5.2

Policies Affecting Human Capital Development

Category	State Policy Description	Pro-Revitalization Features
Early Childhood and Pre-K Education	Provides access to and financial support for pre-K and early childhood education.	Programs maximize the availability and financial support for quality pre-K and early childhood education in low-income areas.
K–12 Education	Supports and regulates K–12 education, including policies governing charter schools, financing educational facilities, and governing mixed- and shared-use school facilities.	Policies provide ample support for quality inclusive urban public education, particularly with respect to lower-income communities—including "cradle to career" programs like the Harlem Children's Zone, programs that provide diverse educational opportunities for students from low-income families and attract diverse families, and programs that maximize opportunities to build educational facilities that help sustain healthy neighborhoods.
Post-Secondary Education	Supports and regulates public higher education, including community colleges and four-year colleges and universities.	Programs provide adequate support for postsecondary education (particularly urban community colleges), maximize access for students from low-income communities, and maximize school–job linkages through employer partnerships, particularly with community colleges.
Workforce Development	Offers job training, retraining, apprenticeships, and other means to improve workforce readiness and job-related skills.	Programs that target workforce needs of inner-city populations and provide meaningful linkages between those populations and job and advancement opportunities in local and regional firms and institutions can maximize job opportunities for residents of lower-income neighborhoods and increase the extent to which they benefit from economic growth.
Local Hiring and Procurement Opportunities	Grants municipal authority to establish local hiring and procurement standards for public projects and for private projects receiving public support.	Programs give flexibility within broad ground rules to municipalities so they can establish local hiring and procurement standards for public projects and for private projects receiving public support.

enforcing regulations, and providing much of the financial support. Workforce development is largely controlled by state labor departments, which also enforce regulations such as prevailing wage laws, which strongly affect the cost of publicly supported construction projects—in some cases unreasonably so. State laws can permit or preempt local governments from enacting minimum wage ordinances or local hiring or purchasing preference programs. But there may be no area in the entire sphere of urban revitalization where the state role is greater—or state policies more fiercely contested—than urban K–12 education.

Prior to the 1990s, urban K–12 education was relatively straightforward, though not without conflict.

The majority of children attended public schools, many Catholic children and a few others went to Catholic parochial schools, and a much smaller number of children went to a mix of private or experimental quasi-public schools, including a handful of Afrocentric schools established in the wake of the civil rights movement.

The picture today is quite different, largely because of two direct outcomes of state law or policy change: the growth of charter schools since first authorized by Minnesota in 1991 and the establishment of school-choice programs. According to the National Alliance for Public Charter Schools, there were 6,824 charter schools educating 2,930,600 pupils in the 2015–2016 school year, slightly less than 6 percent of all K–12 pupils nationally. Charter schools are, however, disproportionately concentrated in urban school districts and make up 26 percent of the combined charter and public-school enrollment in Newark, New Jersey; 27 percent in Cleveland, Ohio; and 49 percent in Detroit, Michigan.

School-choice programs have also proliferated, with different models adopted by different states. Although scale and criteria vary widely, 31 states offer at least one school choice option, and a reasonable estimate would suggest that around 1 million students participate in a school-choice program, disproportionately so in urban districts. Nearly 20 percent of Detroit's students go to suburban schools under Michigan's school choice program, for instance.

The power that states exert over the structure of K–12 education is reinforced by their control over the purse strings.

State law governs every detail of both charter and choice programs, plus much of what takes place in public schools: Whether to permit charter schools at all and under what conditions, how many to authorize, how much money to give them, what criteria they must meet, and under what conditions they can be closed down are all state prerogatives. The same is even more true for choice programs, where local school districts, municipalities, and their residents are either beneficiaries or victims, depending on one's perspective. These are highly contested issues, which have often pitted residents against one another, and residents against school boards or local officials. Finally, state requirements such as mandatory testing further drive the content and structure of public-school education.

In addition to their role in human capital development, schools are often important neighborhood anchors; the quality or perceived quality of education options has a major effect on property values and on many households' choice to move into or remain in a city or neighborhood. Determining which state policies promote urban revitalization and which work against it, however—particularly with respect to charter schools and school choice—is not a straightforward matter. Support of these measures and opposition to them are often driven by ideological, normative, or religious grounds, and this question is also bound up with the level of state financial support for K–12 education, whatever form it may take.

Ultimately, the two criteria to test whether state policies for K–12 education support urban revitalization are whether they lead to better pupil outcomes, particularly with respect to children and youths from low-income areas and communities of color, and whether they strengthen neighborhood housing markets by influencing household decisions to remain in or move into urban neighborhoods. In this light, there is no inherent reason that state policies to authorize charter schools or school choice are necessarily inimical to urban revitalization. With respect to the second criterion in particular, as household location decisions are fundamentally matters of consumer choice, it would seem logical on its face that offering greater consumer choice with respect to K–12 education would be beneficial. It is hardly that simple, however, and the issue of student outcomes is even more complex.

The power that states exert over the structure of K–12 education is reinforced by their control over the purse strings. The financing of urban public education—and the disparities in resources between urban and suburban school districts—has been a highly visible public policy issue for decades. With political calls for change largely stymied, lawsuits demanding additional resources for urban or high-poverty school districts have been filed in all but six of the nation's states since the 1970s. Those fighting to change school funding formulas have prevailed in slightly more than half of those cases.

Teachers, parents, and students march outside of Manzanita Community School in Oakland, California, at a 2019 protest of limited public school funding resulting in large part from the state's 1978 cap on property taxes, which restricts local revenues. A 2020 ballot proposition to revise the law failed. *Source: Jeff Chiu/Associated Press.*

School funding disparities among the states vary in the extreme—both overall and with respect to how much they compensate either for the resource disparities of urban school districts or the compensatory needs of high-poverty districts (which are largely the same). In 2014, half of states provided less than $6,000 in state aid per pupil, while 11 provided over $8,000; amounts ranged from a low of $3,165 per pupil in South Dakota to a high of $16,996 in Vermont, where a single statewide levy covers almost the entire cost of educating the state's children.

The variation in how state funds are distributed is as pronounced as the variation in the overall levels of state support. A 2016 analysis of state funding for low-poverty and high-poverty school districts found that, on a per-pupil basis, Minnesota provided 33 percent more money and New Jersey 24 percent more money to high-poverty districts; by contrast, Illinois and Nevada respectively provided *less* aid to high-poverty districts than to affluent ones (Baker et al. 2016).

Adequate funding is not in itself a sufficient condition to create successful education outcomes in distressed urban schools, but it is a necessary condition. In New Jersey, where state Supreme Court decisions have redirected state educational resources toward high-poverty urban school districts on a large scale, research suggests that student outcomes have significantly improved in many though not all of those districts (Walker et al. 2007). Few states address the larger issues affecting school outcomes, though, and in particular fail to ameliorate the deleterious effects of the economic and racial segregation of so many urban public schools. The impacts of the COVID-19 pandemic on urban public schools and their students are likely to be long-lasting.

In 2019, New Jersey Governor Phil Murphy announced the state's second round of Preschool Education Expansion Aid (PEEA) funding, which provided $27 million to 33 school districts, including Eatontown Public School District, that had never received state aid for preschool before. *Source: GovPhilMurphy/NJ Governor's Office.*

Less contested but equally important is the availability of high-quality early childhood education or pre-K programs. The importance of strong pre-K programs, particularly for children from low-income backgrounds and neighborhoods, is well established. To the extent these programs exist, states play a central role in both authorizing and supporting them; states cover around one-third of the cost of pre-K programs nationally, and the federal Head Start program covers most of the rest.

The funding and prevalence of pre-K education vary widely from state to state. In 2017, Vermont and Florida provided universal pre-K, and virtually all children in those places participated. The same was true in the District of Columbia, which exercises many powers of statehood in this regard, though it's not technically a state. At the other extreme, six states provided no support whatsoever for pre-K education, and nationally two out of three children aged three and four are not enrolled in any form of pre-K education. Every state should provide funds for high-quality pre-K education for all children from low-income families, to develop human capital and foster equity.

In the long run, no system to develop human capital among community residents can succeed unless well-functioning pre-K programs and K–12 schools— public, charter, or otherwise—generate good educational outcomes for the community's children and serve as a springboard to future job opportunities or higher education. While most people look to local educators to generate such outcomes, schools and the educational outcomes for their students are driven by a fiscal, legal, and programmatic framework established by state government to an extraordinary extent. State laws and policies govern far more areas than have been addressed in the foregoing discussion, including broad power over educational budgets, curricula, proficiency testing, and other matters—many of which are matters of recurrent controversy. Those laws and policies often leave much to be desired as a starting point for urban revitalization.

Although state laws and policies related to human capital development may not affect local efforts in other areas as powerfully as they do K–12 education, those laws and policies are pervasive across the board. Most public postsecondary education options available to urban youth are under direct or indirect state control, including state four-year colleges and universities as well as community colleges, which may be run by state, regional, or county entities but are generally subject to state regulation and largely state funded. State labor departments manage workforce development activities, while the 2014 Workforce Innovation and Opportunity Act, the principal federal program for workforce development, provides funds

States can strengthen workforce outcomes by incorporating equitable strategies into both vocational training and employer incentive programs. *Source: BartCo/Getty Images/E+.*

to the states, which then pass them on to local boards. These Workforce Development Boards are, however, still subject to the provisions of a state plan submitted to the federal government spelling out how funds will be spent. States also impose often-onerous licensing requirements that control access to many trades, professions, and business opportunities, disproportionately affecting lower-income communities and individuals. For example, it takes 2,100 hours of training and costs thousands of dollars to become a cosmetologist in South Dakota or Iowa (Carpenter et al. 2021).

States can play a valuable role in strengthening workforce outcomes by incorporating equitable strategies into their programs. Those strategies include building comprehensive, long-term partnerships with major employers (particularly major anchor institutions) and with smaller employers in major opportunity sectors, integrating employer-based skill requirements into the K–12 and post-secondary educational system and workforce training programs, maximizing hiring of local residents, creating apprenticeship and on-the-job training programs, eliminating burdensome and unnecessary licensing requirements, and building career ladders that allow residents ongoing opportunities to gain further skills and promotions.

States have not yet played a significant role in expanding cities' ability to work with developers,

contractors, trade unions, and employers to craft programs that provide for local hiring, training, and similar matters. This condition reflects a preference for the status quo among construction unions, contractors, and developers, and it could change for the worse. As municipalities have sought to address these issues locally, opposition has grown in some states. A bill barring cities from imposing local hiring requirements was signed by Ohio Governor John Kasich in May 2016, while legislatures in Louisiana and Tennessee have introduced similar legislation.

Finally, state policies governing incarceration—including sentencing, bail terms, conditions of incarceration, and opportunities for the formerly incarcerated when they return to their communities—powerfully impact opportunities for residents of distressed communities to build human capital and benefit from their cities' revitalization. The extent to which incarcerated people can obtain education, skills, and support while in prison; and the opportunities available for them on release, are equity issues directly related to the human capital side of urban revitalization. States' track records here are mixed, although positive efforts exist in some places. New Jersey, for instance, has rethought many of its workforce programs around reentry issues, while Iowa offers a tax credit for employers who hire formerly incarcerated individuals.

CHAPTER 6
Embedding Inclusion and Equity in Revitalization

First Fridays in Oakland, California, draw diverse crowds to a rapidly changing city that is grappling with the challenge of how to further equitable revitalization. *Source: Sergio Ruiz.*

A central question underlies the entire subject of urban revitalization: Who is it for? As many American cities began to experience a revival following the Great Recession, the recognition that it does not benefit everyone alike has grown. Instead, cities have become increasingly polarized, with growing numbers of both affluent and poor residents—and fewer in the middle. The landscape of America's urban revival is characterized by inequality.

While some neighborhoods—many in cities like Washington, DC, or New York, and far fewer in legacy cities like Cleveland, Ohio, or Baltimore, Maryland—have revived or gentrified, many more have declined. Outside a handful of economically reviving cities like Seattle, Washington, the economic and fiscal resource gap between central cities and their suburban surroundings is as wide as ever. Cities have more poor and more wealthy neighborhoods but fewer middle-income ones. Black neighborhoods, many already victimized by subprime lending and foreclosure in the recent past, have steadily declined relative to predominantly white neighborhoods in the same cities. The income gap between white and Black residents of older cities has grown steadily wider since 2000. Moreover, as jobs have grown in reviving older cities, few are going to city residents and more to commuters. In many cities, the number of city residents holding jobs, whether inside or outside the city, is declining.

These examples, to which many more could be added, illustrate how unevenly the benefits of revitalization are distributed. Even if revitalization does not make the conditions of disadvantaged residents objectively worse, if benefits are not more equitably distributed the outcome is likely to be greater inequality and polarization, which undermine civic cohesion and social capital. Moreover, growing research supports the proposition that more equitable patterns of development are not only compatible with economic growth but also likely to enhance it. This is true both for countries and for American metropolitan areas (Cingano 2014; Benner and Pastor 2012).

The inequities that have emerged are not race-neutral; indeed, to paraphrase Kendi, nothing is race-neutral in American society (2019). In city after city, Black residents and their neighborhoods have seen little gain from revitalization. Indeed, as some parts of cities like Baltimore, Cleveland, or Philadelphia, Pennsylvania, have prospered, many Black neighborhoods have stagnated or as often declined.

The particular reasons for these trends are complex and manifold, beginning with longstanding patterns of racial segregation and discrimination. Historical and ongoing discrimination in lending and real estate practices, as well as the allocation of public resources, have handicapped Black neighborhoods for generations. Making things worse, at the beginning of the millennium, many of these neighborhoods were specifically targeted by subprime lending, leading to widespread foreclosures and disinvestment during and after the Great Recession. Strategies to ensure equitable neighborhood outcomes must explicitly acknowledge these longstanding dynamics—many of which persist in the present—and address them directly and deliberately.

The "Pavement to Parks" program in Seattle, Washington, converts underutilized street sections into vibrant public amenities, such as the South Park Seattle Library Sitting Area, which was installed in this largely Latinx neighborhood in 2018. *Source: Seattle Department of Transportation.*

Much of the social and racial polarization in reviving cities has centered on the issue of gentrification, or the transformation of formerly lower-income neighborhoods by more affluent in-migrants, leading to higher house prices and potential displacement. An extended discussion of gentrification is well beyond the scope of this report, but it is important to note that the concept has become a stand-in symbol for inequality and powerlessness among existing residents, even in cities where actual gentrification is modest compared to the extent of simultaneous neighborhood decline and impoverishment, as in Detroit. Indeed, in some quarters, this conflation has led to a backlash against revitalization generally, on the premise that the two are inseparable—or even that revitalization is little more than a cover for gentrification (Saunders 2018). Whatever the actual extent of gentrification in a community, these concerns point out the extent to which revival can easily lead to inequitable outcomes, if not accompanied by intentional public-sector strategies of inclusion and equity.

Much of the social and racial polarization in reviving cities has centered on the issue of gentrification, or the transformation of formerly lower-income neighborhoods by more affluent in-migrants, leading to higher house prices and potential displacement.

Regional imbalances in benefits and opportunities for residents can lead to the same patterns of exclusion and inequality in central cities. Suburban areas have historically benefited from the exclusionary patterns that concentrated low-income households and communities of color in central cities, while leaving the individual cities to address poverty and racial inequities largely on their own. Change in this respect is unlikely to happen without intentional state action.

What do we mean by inclusion and equity? As discussed in chapter 1, these are the processes by which revitalization, rather than benefiting the few, benefits the entire city, particularly lower-income households and communities of color. "Benefit" in this context means that these residents are not harmed by revitalization, and that revival leads to greater opportunity for decent jobs, prosperity, and livable neighborhoods with access to goods and services for a decent quality of life. These can be seen as the concrete dimensions of equity and inclusion, but there is another dimension as well: the extent to which all people—and, again, in particular the city's lower-income residents and its communities of color—share in the process as well as the fruits of revitalization. They should not be seen as the passive beneficiaries of the city's largesse but rather as active participants in the process of making decisions about their city's future.

Given the powerful tendency of market-based strategies to favor the already successful, cities are unlikely to realize any of these benefits without intentional strategies for equity and inclusion. Seeming neutrality in policy perpetuates inequitable outcomes. Public strategies for more inclusive or equitable growth require that state policy play a central role; if states adopt policies vis-à-vis local government that actively further equitable, inclusive revitalization and use those rules to impose conditions for access to state funds or authorized powers, they can both support municipalities seeking to infuse greater equity into their revitalization and move reluctant municipalities in that direction. Conversely, the absence of such explicit policies will inevitably undermine local efforts at inclusion and equity, empower those hostile or indifferent to such efforts, and allow historic inequities to continue flourishing.

Inclusion does not exist apart from the elements of revitalization described earlier; it is instead a way to approach those elements and to better design the ground rules that govern them. For example, state economic development incentives could prioritize projects that create the best jobs for community residents, particularly those without college degrees, and that incorporate comprehensive Community Benefit Agreements. State housing policies could be designed to integrate affordable housing into market-building strategies by encouraging mixed-income development. Table 6.1 offers more examples of how state policies can be designed to foster greater inclusion in each area, though this is not, of course, an exhaustive list.

The overarching state goal should be, as in medicine, to first, do no harm. Many state policies, while theoretically neutral, in practice increase inequality and the likelihood that lower-income people and

Table 6.1

Representative State Policies to Further Inclusivity in Revitalization

Category	Representative Inclusivity Policies
Fiscal Capacity and Service Delivery	• Progressive tax policies benefiting lower-income households • State aid criteria reflecting municipal inclusion policies • Property tax circuit-breakers to protect low-income homeowners, both generally and particularly in areas with rising property values
Economic Competitiveness	• Criteria for economic development incentives that include local hiring, particularly of workers without bachelor's or higher degrees • Small business support programs targeted to lower-income communities and to communities of color • Transportation policies that maximize increased access to job opportunities for low-income communities • Redevelopment laws to ensure that low-income families in redevelopment areas are not harmed
Healthy Real Estate Market	• Policies that encourage mixed-income housing development, particularly in areas of opportunity such as near transit stations or adjacent to major employers • Programs to increase access to sustainable homeownership for lower-income households in urban neighborhoods • Legal authority for effective municipal and community-based strategies to address vacant properties and problem rental properties
Healthy Neighborhoods and Quality of Life	• Programs to support open space and greening in lower-income communities • Programs to stabilize struggling middle neighborhoods • Support for restructuring police functions around more community-based strategies
Human Capital Development	• Adequate state aid to urban school districts • Charter school and other school-choice programs, conditional on evidence that the schools clearly provide comparable or greater benefits to children from lower-income households and distressed neighborhoods than existing public schools do—without shifting undue burdens or costs onto the urban public-school systems • Strong, systematic linkages between economic development programs and workforce development programs • Legal authority for effective local hiring and community benefits programs • Strong educational and support programs for incarcerated persons and strong reentry programs for their return to their communities

California Governor Gavin Newsom signs into law the right for family childcare providers to unionize—a major equity win for a workforce dependent upon state subsidies and comprised mainly of women of color. *Source: Robert Durell.*

their communities will be excluded from the benefits of revitalization. These deceptively neutral policies may include:

- regressive tax policies;
- transportation approaches that prioritize new construction over maintenance and upgrading of existing facilities, highways over public transportation, and rural or suburban areas over urban ones;
- housing policies that concentrate affordable housing in high-poverty urban neighborhoods; and
- education policies that directly or indirectly provide greater benefit for more affluent, better educated households than lower-income households.

Exacerbating inequality does not require deliberate intent. Many laws are enacted to serve a particular purpose with little awareness of unintended consequences, and once on the books they tend to stay there. We do not believe that the state of Michigan's notoriously regressive charter school law was enacted with deliberate intent to harm Detroit's struggling low-income children, but that effect could easily have been predicted. Since the consequences become apparent, moreover, the state has taken no action to change those policies or mitigate their inequitable outcomes.

State policies to further inclusivity in urban revitalization are not the same as policies to ameliorate the

disadvantages of poverty, although there is considerable overlap between the two. Provision of subsidized housing is critically important to any serious strategy for improving the quality of life of low-income households and alleviating poverty, but it is not in and of itself an urban revitalization strategy. Policies that locate affordable housing in areas of opportunity, however, can be inclusive revitalization strategies—particularly where such housing is pursued through mixed-income, mixed-use developments that simultaneously help build stronger markets or that enable low-income families to move to those areas with housing vouchers. Similarly, if the Housing Choice Voucher program, which provides a federal subsidy for low-income families to live in privately owned housing, were made an entitlement program similar to the federal SNAP food program—rather than the current lottery, under which only one out of four or five eligible households receives benefits—that would benefit low-income families immeasurably and also benefit neighborhood outcomes by increasing family and residential stability.

Every state's revitalization policies should include an inclusivity framework that evaluates state policies—including laws, regulations, and appropriations—for their effect on inclusion and equity. Such a framework can also work well in reverse by examining anti-poverty and social support programs from an urban revitalization perspective and by exploring how they may be used to help further urban revitalization without losing track of their primary goal.

CHAPTER 7
Toward a Reform Agenda

When developing an agenda to reform state policy to promote urban revitalization, no one solution will suit every city. States vary widely in their legal frameworks and governance structures, their political cultures and histories, and their concern for cities and their issues. There are "machine" states, where key decisions are tightly controlled by a small political elite, and states in which decision-making is a blur of changing coalitions and interests. There are also, of course, so-called red states, blue states, and a few purple ones in the middle of the political spectrum.

Woodward Avenue in Detroit, Michigan, demarcates declining and thriving neighborhoods in a city known for its rocky path to revitalization. *Source: Johnny Miller/Unequal Scenes.*

As advocates frame policy agendas to further urban revitalization in their states, understanding the state's unique set of realities becomes key to whether those agendas are likely to advance. Political climate is particularly important; in many states, profound differences exist between the politics of state government (particularly state legislatures) and those of major cities—a divide that fosters an ongoing tug-of-war between the two, often leading to state preemption of municipal ordinances.

While partisan conflict is often just below the surface in today's polarized political climate, and some hot-button issues affecting urban revitalization have become partisan battlegrounds (like charter schools), it is still possible to find common ground. Urban Republican mayors tend to focus on many of the same issues as their Democratic counterparts, and many of their cities' most important issues are far from partisan. Advocates have been able to find broad support on both sides of the aisle to address vacant and problem properties, including the creation of strong land bank entities in states as diverse as New York, Georgia, and Nebraska. Effective advocacy lies in understanding what is possible in the near term, while doing the arduous work needed to gradually expand the range of the possible in the long term.

In addition to understanding the state government's political climate, advocates must consider the distribution of power and influence affecting that climate, particularly in state legislatures. While it is the legislators who ultimately vote, a diverse network of organizations influence their decisions. This substratum includes trade and professional associations, paid and volunteer lobbyists, issue-based organizations, ad hoc coalitions, and sometimes more shadowy individuals behind the scenes. Each actor brings their own agenda, and their role is to advocate on behalf of that agenda or block things that they see as harming members or constituents. Many people who act on behalf of these organizations are likely to be State House fixtures: people who know the legislators, their senior staff, and key figures in the state administration. Legislators vote, but the substratum often determines what they vote on.

In contrast to the U.S. Congress, with its extensively staffed committees and support entities like the Congressional Budget Office, legislative expertise and staff support in most states is often very limited. This is particularly true in the 15 states where term limits have created revolving doors, in which legislators often must step down by the time they have begun to develop real expertise—or even before. As a result, state legislators everywhere depend heavily on outside sources for information and advice, and they are likely to depend most heavily on people they have come to know and trust, rightly or wrongly.

A strong land bank entity can effectively rehabilitate vacant or problem properties, such as in Cleveland, Ohio—often with bipartisan support at the state level. *Source: Courtesy of the Cuyahoga Land Bank.*

This arrangement also means that advocates must often assume a proactive role in not only promoting ideas but also actually drafting legislation.

As that suggests, legislative impact at the state level is ultimately about relationships. In contrast to federal elected officials, meeting with state legislators and senior state administration officials is often not difficult. Advocates must do so and build ongoing relationships with key people who influence urban policy issues. An important part of that process is finding legislators, preferably with standing in the majority caucus, who not only support one's proposals but will champion them as personal priorities, actively pushing for them and negotiating with colleagues to build support for passage. Getting bills introduced is easy; getting them enacted is hard. In the average year, more than 109,000 bills are introduced in state legislatures, but only a tiny fraction become law (Erickson 2017). Without champions, few bills of any real significance ever see the light of day.

Specific proposals put forth by advocates of urban revitalization will vary based on the cities' needs and the state's political culture and fiscal climate. In any case, advocates should consider grounding their proposals around the following five underlying principles for how state decision-makers should think about urban revitalization.

Target Areas of Greatest Need

"Neutral" policies are not neutral when the playing field is unlevel; they benefit those who begin with the advantageous position. The metropolitan playing field is neither level nor neutral, and cities face multiple disadvantages compared to many suburbs. They are forced to address disproportionate problems of poverty and disadvantage with severely limited fiscal resources, while urban redevelopment is slower, more complex, and more expensive than suburban greenfield development.

Thus, when a state provides the same or less financial assistance to high-poverty and low-poverty school districts or when it offers a comparable package of economic development incentives to both affluent suburban areas and central cities, those policies perpetuate the advantages of more affluent areas and exacerbate the economic disparity between them and economically stressed central cities.

Legislative impact at the state level is ultimately about relationships. In contrast to federal elected officials, meeting with state legislators and senior state administration officials is often not difficult.

If one believes that the cities do not matter, neutral policies might seem like a legitimate, albeit unfortunate, policy choice. But the evidence is to the contrary: Cities are deeply relevant to the future health and vitality of their regions and their states. Metropolitan areas, made up of large central cities and the surrounding suburban areas from which people commute to work, drive state economies. Ohio's seven largest metro areas are home to 71 percent of its population, 76 percent of its jobs, and 80 percent of the state's gross domestic product. While core cities comprise only a portion of metropolitan economic and population bases, regional prosperity closely follows the health of a central city. Research has consistently shown a close connection between central city strength and broader metropolitan prosperity, and between central city and suburban job growth (Voith 1998). Other research has shown that central city decline and wide gaps between the economic health of cities and suburbs are associated with slow metropolitan income growth (Benner and Pastor 2012).

Central cities contain key institutions—particularly universities and medical centers—likely to play an important role in future economic growth. These major anchor institutions serve as both economic engines

and invaluable intellectual and creative resources, generating thousands of jobs and billions of dollars in economic activity. Indeed, the ability to capitalize on these urban assets may be the single most important factor determining the future economic prosperity of a cluster of northeastern and midwestern states, including Pennsylvania, Ohio, and Michigan.

States can enable those institutions to grow as statewide economic engines—or they can sit on the sidelines, in which case the state and its residents are likely to miss out on significant growth opportunities. States also spend billions of dollars each year on their older cities in the forms of school aid, municipal aid, public assistance, infrastructure investments, and workforce development funds—all costs that rise with the impoverishment of these cities and their residents. In the absence of revitalization, these costs will continue to drain state finances. States should spend money to lay the groundwork for economic recovery, not to enable continued decline.

Perhaps the most compelling argument for a constructive state role in urban revitalization is, ironically, the extent to which cities have become manifestly more attractive as both business locations and places to live than at any time in the recent past. It is not likely that the COVID-19 pandemic will lead to fundamental change in that regard in coming years. While cities still urgently need the support of their state governments, the environment for that support is fundamentally different than in the past. Thus, in contrast to the 1970s

Newark's University Hospital is the primary teaching hospital for Rutgers New Jersey Medical School and an anchor institution for both the state and local community, generating major economic activity in the area. *Source: Keith B. Bratcher, Jr.*

and 1980s, when revitalization efforts were at best holding actions attempting to prevent further urban decline in the face of powerful anti-urban pressures, the wave of urban investment and in-migration over the past 20 years means that revitalization now holds real potential to transform the economic character and quality of life in America's older industrial cities. Whether such change will happen, however, is far from a foregone conclusion; the point is that revitalization represents a realistic—perhaps once-in-a-lifetime—opportunity. The wave will not last forever. States will play a significant role in determining whether the opportunity ahead is realized or lost.

Think Regionally

A targeted approach to central cities is essential, but it cannot take place in a vacuum. Cities and their suburban surroundings form a single, integrated economic unit. Housing markets, job markets, transportation, and business networks all operate with little regard for municipal and county boundaries. Regions are, however, governmentally fragmented. Allegheny County, Pennsylvania, which contains Pittsburgh, has

133 separate incorporated municipalities with a total population of roughly 1.2 million. Despite some growth in regional cooperation on issues such as public transportation or economic development, competition for scarce resources and development opportunities among municipalities and counties in metropolitan areas is intense. In contrast to the private sector, where competition may be productive, public-sector competition tends to foster zero-sum outcomes, along with a "race to the bottom," in which municipalities compete by offering excessive business incentives (Chirinko and Wilson 2008; Mast 2020).

Some regional initiatives that directly engage issues of race or poverty are often politically controversial. Advocates should seek opportunities to promote greater cooperation and coordination across municipal and county boundaries in areas that can improve delivery of public services and lead to greater equity between municipalities in areas like transportation, economic development, housing, or land use. At a time when racial and economic equity are increasingly central to the national political agenda, decision makers may be more sensitive to the suburbs' role in fostering inequity. As a result, the sorts of regional strategies that can contribute to acknowledging and addressing concerns about equity may receive a more responsive hearing than in the past.

Regional agencies can help provide the capacity to plan and execute activities that foster revitalization and regional equity, particularly in regions containing multiple small cities where strong local capacity may be beyond the reach of individual cities. Where strong Metropolitan Planning Organizations (MPOs) or Councils of Government (COGs) already exist, the state should support such organizations, building their resources and strengthening their powers. Elsewhere, states can provide legal frameworks for creating new regional bodies with the ability to affect regional decision-making, as New York State did by creating its Regional Economic Development Councils in 2011.

Break Down Silos

The habit of treating each area of government activity as not only distinct but largely disconnected from others (sometimes called "siloing") is self-evidently problematic and one of the practices most resistant to change in both state and local government. Even the most casual observer can easily grasp that transportation affects land use, that economic development affects housing markets, and that policies should be coordinated and integrated. Where they are not, conflicts and inconsistencies between policies, not to mention inefficient use of limited resources, are likely to be common.

Despite the self-evident dysfunctionality of governmental siloing, it persists because of the powerful centrifugal tendencies of government agencies' organizational structures. These inherent tendencies are reinforced by "a variety of internal and external forces, including conflicts among the missions of individual agencies, human imperfection, and competition for scarce resources. Every agency contains an internal mix of these variables that make its own units slow or reluctant to act" (Pendall et al. 2013).

Silos exist in both state and local government. Though states should use their resources to encourage cities to break down silos and fashion multifaceted revitalization strategies, they are often even more silo-bound than local governments. Critical functions affecting urban revitalization are also increasingly in the hands of independent or quasi-independent entities at the state level, such as housing finance agencies, economic development authorities, or even nongovernmental entities such as JobsOhio, a private nonprofit entity created in 2011 by the Kasich administration to "drive job creation and new capital investment in Ohio through business attraction, retention, and expansion efforts" (JobsOhio.com). Delegation of state powers to such entities is often justified on the grounds that it facilitates interaction with private-sector players and delivery of financial products, but it can also make coordinated state-level efforts more difficult and complicate state efforts to encourage equitable urban revitalization.

Many efforts by state or local governments to break down silos and foster integrated strategies have tended to be driven by a particular mayor or governor and take the form of working groups or other ad hoc initiatives, rather than being institutionalized as a formal, ongoing part of government. As a result, these efforts tend to wither or disappear when a new chief executive arrives—or sometimes even under the same one, if administration priorities shift enough. Such initiatives rarely lead to meaningful change, particularly as permanent program or department heads, well aware of the fleeting nature of political leadership, simply bide their time until the initiative runs out of steam.

Support Cities' Own Efforts

Ultimately, cities must take the responsibility for their future. While "creatures of the state," they are nonetheless creatures with the ability to act. They have direct responsibility for their citizens' welfare and the duty to make decisions to drive their future. State governments, moreover, need to recognize that their wisdom is rarely great enough to substitute for hands-on engagement by local officials with greater knowledge of local conditions. While state government may have to intervene in extreme situations such as financial crises, those situations are rare. Even then, the outcomes of most such experiences do not support the proposition that state officials necessarily know better than local ones.

State urban policies often place narrow and sometimes arbitrary constraints on local discretion; alternatively, they impose state preferences on local governments, even where local officials consider them inconsistent with the city's needs or goals. While state leaders may believe that they are preventing waste and abuse by irresponsible local officials, sustainable

revitalization cannot be imposed from outside; it must be the product of active engagement by local stakeholders, enabled by a supportive state. In the long run, state policies that hinder local officials, nongovernmental organizations, and engaged residents from framing creative, locally specific strategies will not advance revitalization.

That said, limits on local capacity—with respect to both the number of professionally trained staff and their expertise—to design and implement effective and inclusive revitalization strategies seriously limits the ability of many cities to carry out successful revitalization activities. Planning, housing, and economic development offices are often understaffed, and staff too often lack the sophisticated skills needed to address the complex, multidimensional challenges their communities face. A few cities have strong networks of community institutions to complement—and sometimes replace—municipal capacity, but most do not. This problem is particularly acute in smaller cities, which often have the most limited municipal capacity as well as the most limited citizen infrastructure.

The answer, then, is not to impose state "solutions" on local governments or to parachute less knowledgeable state officials into city halls. Rather, cities should use state resources to build local capacity. In smaller cities and towns, it may be most productive to build up strong regional organizations that provide services to municipalities lacking the resources to offer their own.

Build in Equity and Inclusivity

Intentional strategies to build equity and inclusivity into revitalization are growing in number but remain the exception rather than the rule. More and more people recognize their importance, but far more determined efforts are needed from all those responsible for revitalization activities. There are many reasons for this; the painful fact is that fostering equity and

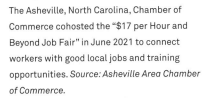

The Asheville, North Carolina, Chamber of Commerce cohosted the "$17 per Hour and Beyond Job Fair" in June 2021 to connect workers with good local jobs and training opportunities. *Source: Asheville Area Chamber of Commerce.*

inclusion is difficult, particularly when income and racial disparities are so great and the burdens of poverty and racism so painful. The underlying drivers of those disparities are well beyond a city's ability to influence by itself, let alone control, and the resources available to cities to address these issues are severely limited.

Even though cities have tools to foster equity and inclusion in their revitalization activities, many choose not to use them as aggressively or effectively as they could. This may stem from an alignment of values between local government officials and developers or other key private sector players, or from local officials' fear that developers or corporations will go elsewhere if required to provide inclusionary housing units or to adhere to local hiring percentages. This reluctance may also simply reflect the extent to which overtaxed local officials find it more difficult to add equity and inclusion to an already demanding agenda.

States should incorporate an equity and inclusivity framework into their policies to guide all activities and financial investments in support of urban revitalization. The state should further commit to ensuring that local governments act to further equity and inclusion in their policies and practices and that state programs themselves, whether addressing economic competitiveness, housing, quality of life or public education, are consistently designed in ways that further equity and inclusion. States should tie the level of their support for individual cities' revitalization

directly to those cities' ability and will to meaningfully further economic and racial equity and inclusion. Beyond establishing that principle, states can take many specific steps:

- Pass legislation to advance equity and inclusion, such as increases to minimum wages or Earned Income Tax Credit levels, or incorporate clear community benefit criteria into the state's economic development and redevelopment incentives.

- Enact legislation giving municipalities clear legal authority to pursue equity and inclusion strategies, such as inclusionary zoning ordinances or local hiring and living wage requirements, for projects receiving discretionary municipal benefits.

- Establish state programs that support equity and inclusion in the revitalization agenda, as outlined previously in table 6.

- Develop equity and inclusion criteria for discretionary state funding, whether general municipal assistance or project-specific support, either as a threshold condition for eligibility or in the form of incentives that trigger higher funding levels for local government.

Fostering equity is about taking concrete steps, not making pronouncements. Those steps should be clear, focused, and enforceable.

CHAPTER 8
Conclusions and Recommendations

Both redevelopment and historical preservation near the Wisconsin State Capitol in Madison have allowed the area to revitalize while maintaining its unique character. *Source: Images-USA/Alamy Stock Photo.*

Each state has its own body of constitutional standards, laws, and programs, as well as its own priorities and political culture. Given the extent of state involvement with urban revitalization, hundreds of different recommendations could be made. This report identifies a smaller number of particularly important ones, while recognizing that some may be more politically feasible in certain states than in others.

Equity and inclusion are fundamental to revitalization, and states have many tools to put them on the agenda. Budgeting frameworks that take race, ethnicity, and gender into account can help states allocate resources more equitably and address historic disparities. State laws and regulations can be assessed according to whether they foster or impede inclusive revitalization, while racial equity impact assessments can help state agencies and legislatures systematically examine how a proposed action or decision will affect various racial and ethnic groups. Such assessments are being used by many cities around the country, including St. Paul, Minnesota. Iowa and Connecticut use such assessments to determine the impact of sentencing laws.

These recommendations are building blocks for advocates working to create an agenda to change their state's policies. They can also help advocates assess the extent to which a state's policies are currently supporting or hindering urban revitalization.

STRENGTHEN FISCAL CAPACITY AND SERVICE DELIVERY

States should allow cities to access a variety of revenue sources—potentially including property, wage, and sales taxes—as well as reasonable user charges, fees, and host benefits. States should consider the following measures.

- Allow municipalities to add a small amount to existing state sales taxes, or dedicate part of state sales taxes collected in distressed municipalities to local revitalization trust funds.
- Enable municipalities to impose rental registration and licensing fees and vacant property registration fees that reflect the cost of municipal activities to regulate and address problem properties.
- Ensure that the municipal share of specialized tax revenues associated with state-regulated industries (such as casinos) reflects the cost of providing services to those facilities and helps address other fiscal imbalances affecting those cities.

States should use need-based formulas to allocate support for school districts and municipal finances, with incentives built into aid formulas to encourage high-quality performance or sustained improvement. State support should incorporate responsible oversight of municipal finances to ensure

The city of Minneapolis, Minnesota, has recently reckoned with its racial equity framework following the 2020 murder of George Floyd, in whose memory community organizers have established a public garden and city square. *Source: Fibonacci Blue/Flickr.*

local government accountability and effectively manage fiscal crises. States should consider the following steps.

- Make state school aid need-based, reflecting the school district's fiscal condition and characteristics of its student body, such as free lunch eligibility.
- Establish municipal aid programs based on municipal fiscal capacity, revenue constraints, and disproportionate demand for local services.
- Create supplemental aid programs, over and above base assistance programs, for municipal governments that achieve revitalization goals and meet or exceed other performance standards.
- Adopt graduated fiscal monitoring systems to track municipal fiscal performance and identify early stages of fiscal distress, along with standards for municipal transparency in budgeting and fiscal reporting.
- Standardize user-friendly formats for providing public information on municipal revenues and expenditures.

FOSTER A ROBUST HOUSING MARKET

States should provide funds for market-building and multifaceted neighborhood revitalization. This will further well-grounded revitalization strategies carried out through public, private, and community partnerships.

- Grant local government flexibility to provide targeted incentives, including tax abatements and/or both project and neighborhood TIF, to address market gaps.
- Provide financial incentives for mixed-income developments in appropriate locations including mortgage financing, subordinated financing, state tax credits, historic tax credits, and state tax credits for home buyers in designated neighborhood investment areas.

The Barack H. Obama Magnet University School in New Haven, Connecticut, is a kindergarten-through fourth grade "lab" school on the Southern Connecticut State University campus, built in partnership between the university and the city's public school district. *Source: JCJ Architecture/Pickard Chilton.*

- Incorporate fair-housing principles into state assistance programs, including mixed-income housing, support for affordable housing in areas of opportunity, and measures that address barriers to building racially and economically integrated communities.

States should provide municipalities with strong tools to address problem properties, including the following.

- Authorize counties and municipalities to create land bank entities, with appropriate powers and dedicated resources.
- Amend tax foreclosure laws to provide alternatives to "tax farming" models of selling tax liens to third-party buyers, including provisions similar to those of Ohio or Michigan, which allow liens or properties to flow directly to land banks.
- Provide clear legal authority for rental licensing and for regular inspections of rental properties.
- Encourage performance-based code enforcement systems and good landlord incentives.
- Authorize vacant property receivership and spot blight eminent domain for vacant properties to ensure productive reuse of properties.

STIMULATE A COMPETITIVE ECONOMY

States should provide economic development incentives that are transparent, efficient, and integrated with local revitalization strategies. Before committing public resources, they should also ensure that they maximize local benefits—particularly to disadvantaged populations and communities—based on rigorous cost-benefit analyses and opportunity-cost evaluations.

- Offer greater incentives for private investment in distressed areas that result in clear and measurable benefits for the lower-income residents of those areas, based on explicit community-benefit and cost-benefit criteria, including opportunity cost analysis.
- Monitor all economic incentives to ensure that the promised community benefits are actually realized and incorporate "clawbacks," to recapture funds spent if incentive targets are not met.
- Enact state incentives to maximize use of federal Opportunity Zone incentives explicitly for projects targeted to areas of need that provide tangible benefits to lower-income area residents.
- Adopt explicit community-benefit criteria for all major state development projects and for all disposition of state properties.

State laws should allow flexible use of redevelopment tools, subject to planning and oversight requirements to ensure they are used productively.

- Provide flexible legal authority for municipal redevelopment activities, including power to issue mortgage and industrial revenue bonds, use eminent domain to take property for redevelopment subject to procedures that protect property owner and resident interests, use project and areawide tax increment financing, create special taxing and improvement districts, and grant property tax abatements tailored to local conditions.
- Require transparent use of redevelopment tools, including regular public reporting by municipalities and quasi-public agencies such as land banks or economic development corporations, and establish state fiscal and substantive tracking of redevelopment activities.
- Provide financial assistance for redevelopment readiness, such as reforming or updating land use regulations and approval procedures, creating property databases, and upgrading local planning and redevelopment capacity.

- Provide support to local governments and community-based organizations in framing effective community benefit agreements for major redevelopment projects, including model agreements and a state platform for monitoring compliance with agreements.

State governments should become facilitators of catalytic local change by building local capacity, providing technical support, and investing in potentially transformative local projects and strategies.

- Establish community revitalization centers of excellence, staffed by highly qualified individuals to both help build the local capacity to design and execute revitalization efforts and enhance the capacity of state officials to provide effective support to local governments' activities.
- Provide funds and technical support for transformative projects likely to have a significant impact on cities' economic or market conditions, by designing competitive programs that challenge local governments to create innovative and integrated programs and communitywide partnerships.
- Create high-capacity technical support teams to assist local governments to obtain approvals and to navigate and leverage federal, state, and private resources to undertake transformative projects.

CULTIVATE HEALTHY NEIGHBORHOODS AND QUALITY OF LIFE

State governments should support historic preservation, parks and open space, and arts and cultural activities in ways that contribute to urban and neighborhood revitalization. This could be through tax credits, grants, and other means to the following ends.

- Support comprehensive and equitable neighborhood revitalization strategies in targeted neighborhoods, such as funding infrastructure improvements to facilitate housing and redevelopment projects and "soft" strategies to build community cohesion and social capital.
- Promote greening to improve and elevate the natural systems of green space, street trees, and waterways that make cities and neighborhoods livable places, and restore urban parks in conjunction with local neighborhood revitalization initiatives.

The Creative Little Garden in New York City's Lower East Side is one of many "pocket parks," redeveloped on small vacant sites by residents of the neighborhoods in which they are situated. *Source: creativelittlegarden/Instagram.*

Residents of Iowa City, Iowa, enjoy the popular annual city-sponsored block party, which draws locals to the Downtown District. *Source: Alan Light/ Wikimedia Commons.*

- Fund partnerships between arts organizations and neighborhood organizations to carry out activities that integrate visual and performing arts with neighborhood revitalization.

BUILD HUMAN CAPITAL

States should build comprehensive, long-term partnerships with employers to integrate their skill requirements into the K–12 and postsecondary educational systems, maximize hiring of local residents, and build career ladders that allow residents ongoing opportunities to gain further skills and promotions.

- Ensure that state training funds—including federal passthrough funds and funds for vocational education—target low-income individuals in need, prioritize areas that require job growth and future hiring, and align with specific employers' hiring needs.

- Ensure that all workforce development programs are integrated with educational support and assistance in removing legal disabilities, and in providing other services to maximize participants' post-training employability and retention.

- Support robust reentry programs for formerly incarcerated individuals returning to their communities, including training, workforce opportunities, and support services in areas such as housing and health.

- Evaluate and amend state occupational licensing requirements where they act as unreasonable barriers to entry, particularly in fields likely to benefit lower-income urban residents.

In the final analysis, the revitalization of America's older cities and towns—and the extent to which that revitalization benefits their lower-income residents and communities of color—depends on multiple factors, many of which are beyond the control of either the cities or their state governments. Yet, as this report shows, the states play a central, even essential, role in making revitalization possible—or, conversely, frustrating local revitalization efforts. This report should encourage public officials and advocates for change to make states more supportive, engaged partners with local governments and other stakeholders in their efforts to make our cities stronger, healthier places for all.

References

Andreason, Stuart, and Ann Carpenter. 2015. *Fragmentation in Workforce Development and Efforts to Coordinate Regional Workforce Development Systems: A Case Study of Challenges in Atlanta and Models for Regional Cooperation from Across the Country*. Atlanta, GA: Federal Reserve Bank of Atlanta.

Baker, Bruce, Danielle Farrie, Theresa Luhm, and David G. Sciarra. 2016. *Is School Funding Fair? A National Report Card*. Newark, NJ: Education Law Center and Rutgers Graduate School of Education.

Bardik, Timothy J. 2019. *Making Sense of Incentives: Taming Business Incentives to Promote Prosperity*. Kalamazoo, MI: W.E. Upjohn Institute for Employment Research.

Benner, Chris, and Manuel Pastor. 2012. Just Growth: Inclusion and Prosperity in America's Metropolitan Regions. New York, NY: Routledge.

Carpenter, Dick M. II, Lisa Knepper, Kyle Sweetland, and Jennifer McDonald. 2021. *License to Work: A National Study of Burdens from Occupational Licensing*. Washington, DC: Institute for Justice.

Chirinko, R.S., and D.J. Wilson. 2008. "State investment tax incentives: A zero-sum game?" *Journal of Public Economics* 92(12): 2362–2384.

Clark, Terry Nichols. 2011. *The City as an Entertainment Machine*. Lanham, MD: Lexington Books.

Cingano, Federico. 2014. *Trends in Income Inequality and its Impact on Economic Growth*. Paris, France: Organization for Economic Cooperation and Development (OECD).

Commonwealth of Pennsylvania. 2008. *Governor's Report on State Performance 2006–2007*. Harrisburg, PA: Commonwealth of Pennsylvania.

Erickson, Brenda. 2017. "Limiting Bill Introductions," *LegisBrief*, Vol. 25, No.23, June 2017, https://www.ncsl.org/research/about-state-legislatures/limiting-bill-introductions.aspx.

Fiscal Policy Institute. 2015. "Addressing the Unintended Consequences of the Property Tax Cap." New York, NY: Fiscal Policy Institute. http://fiscalpolicy.org/wp-content/uploads/2015/06/Addressing-Unintended-Consequences-of-Property-Tax-Cap-06-10-2015.pdf.

Florida, Richard. 2002. *The Rise of the Creative Class*. New York, NY: Basic Books.

Frug, Gerald E., and David J. Barron. 2008. *City Bound: How States Stifle Urban Innovation*. Ithaca, NY: Cornell University Press.

Jobs Ohio. "About Us." https://www.jobsohio.com/about-us/.

Kendi, Ibram X. 2019. *How to Be an Anti-Racist*. New York, NY: One World.

Mallach, Alan, and Diane Sterner. 2008. "New Jersey and its Cities: An Agenda for Urban Revitalization." Trenton, NJ: Housing and Community Development Network of New Jersey.

Mallach, Alan, and Lavea Brachman. 2013. *Regenerating America's Legacy Cities*. Policy focus report. Cambridge, MA: Lincoln Institute of Land Policy.

Mast, Evan. 2020. "Race to the bottom? Local tax break competition and business location." *American Economic Journal: Applied Economics* 12(1): 288–317.

McFarland, Christiana K., and Christopher Hoene. 2015. *Cities and State Fiscal Structure 2015*. Washington, DC: National League of Cities.

Nurin, Tara. 2015. "The List: Camden Banks on Millions in Tax Subsidies to Help Fund Its Future." *NJ Spotlight*. October 6. https://www.njspotlight.com/2015/10/15-10-05-the-list-camden-banks-on-millions-in-tax-subsidies-to-fund-its-future.

Pendall, Rolf, Sandra Rosenbloom, Diane K. Levy, Elizabeth Oo, Gerrit Knaap, Arnab Chakraborty, and Jason Sartori. 2013. "Can Federal Efforts Advance Federal and Local De-Siloing?" In *Lessons from the HUD-EPA-DOT Partnership for Sustainable Communities.* Washington, DC: Urban Institute.

Peters, Alan, and Peter Fisher. 2004. "The Failures of Economic Development Incentives." *Journal of the American Planning Association* 70(1): 27–37.

Salam, Reihan. 2014. "How the Suburbs Got Poor—Places that Thrived in the Era of Two-Parent Families Are Struggling Today." *Slate*. September 4. https://slate.com/news-and-politics/2014/09/poverty-in-the-suburbs-places-that-thrived-in-the-era-of-two-parent-families-are-struggling-today.html.

Safeguard Properties. "Online Vacant Property Registration Database." https://safeguardproperties.com/vacant-property-registration.

Saunders, Pete. 2018. "The Scales of Gentrification" *Planning Magazine.* December.

Voith, Richard. 1998. "Do suburbs need cities?" *Journal of Regional Science* 38 (3): 445–464.

Walczak, Jared. 2019. *Local Income Taxes in 2019*. Washington DC: The Tax Foundation.

Walker, Elaine M., Charles Achilles, and Carol Frances. 2007. "The Impact of the 1998 Abbott v. Burke Decision on Educational Progress in New Jersey High Poverty Districts: What have we learned?" Berkeley, CA: Chief Justice Earl Warren Institute on Race, Ethnicity and Diversity at the University of California, Berkeley, School of Law.

Wilkinson, Mike. 2016. "Revenue tools help Toledo survive through tough times." *Bridge Magazine*. May 17. www.mlive.com/politics/index.ssf/2016/05/revenue_tools_help_toledo_surv.html.

Acknowledgments

This report has had a long gestation period, beginning with conversations with Lavea Brachman of the Brookings Institution at the time when she led the Greater Ohio Policy Center, with Peter Kasabach of New Jersey Future, and with others, which led to a working paper that the Lincoln Institute released in 2017. The initial impetus to turn the working paper into a Policy Focus Report came roughly two years ago from Jessie Grogan at the Lincoln Institute, who has shepherded it through the process from that point onward.

It has been a pleasure working with her, as it has been working on this report with my colleagues Akilah Watkins and Rob Finn at the Center for Community Progress. Valuable feedback on the draft came from Flora Arabo, Enterprise Community Partners; Wade Beltramo, New York State Conference of Mayors; Alan Berube, Brookings Institution; Karen Black, May 8 Consulting; Ben Forman, MassINC; Alison Goebel, Greater Ohio Policy Center; Chris Hackbarth and Tony Minghine, Michigan Municipal League; Nick Hamilton, Good City Company; Bambie Hayes-Brown, Georgia ACT; Peter Kasabach, New Jersey Future; Mark Kudlowitz, LISC; RJ McGrail, Lincoln Institute of Land Policy; Stacie Reidenbaugh, 10,000 Friends of Pennsylvania; Victor Rubin and Sarah Treuhaft, PolicyLink; and Scott Wolf, Grow Smart Rhode Island.

ABOUT THE AUTHOR

Alan Mallach is a senior fellow at the Center for Community Progress and a visiting professor at the Pratt Institute Graduate Center for Planning and the Environment. He has coauthored two Lincoln Institute Policy Focus Reports, *Regenerating America's Legacy Cities* (2013) and *The Empty House Next Door* (2018), and edited the book *Rebuilding America's Legacy Cities: New Directions for the Industrial Heartland* (2012). His latest book, *The Divided City: Poverty and Prosperity in Urban America,* was published in 2018.

POLICY FOCUS REPORT SERIES

The Policy Focus Report series is published by the Lincoln Institute of Land Policy to address timely public policy issues relating to land use, land markets, and property taxation. Each report is designed to bridge the gap between theory and practice by combining research findings, case studies, and contributions from scholars in a variety of academic disciplines, and information from professional practitioners, local officials, and citizens in diverse communities.